# Good Living
# Is Like Good Cooking

## and Other Suggestions
## for Right Living

by
*Matthew F. Kohmescher, S.M.*

**Paulist Press**
**New York/Mahwah**

The Scripture quotations contained herein are from the Revised Standard Ver
sion of the Bible, copyrighted 1946, 1952 and 1971 by the Division of Christian
Education of the National Council of the Churches of Christ in the U.S.A.,
and used by permission. All rights reserved.

The edited paper entitled "Good Morality is Like Good Cooking" by Kathy J.
Riepenhoff, which appears in Chapter 1 is reprinted by permission of the au-
thor.

## Library of Congress Cataloging-in-Publication Data

Kohmescher, Matthew F.
   Good morality is like good cooking.

   Bibliography: p.
   1. Christian ethics—Catholic authors.   I. Title.
BJ1249.K64   1986      241'.042      86-25500
ISBN 0-8091-2856-X (pbk.)

Published by Paulist Press
997 Macarthur Boulevard
Mahwah, New Jersey 07430

Printed and bound in the
United States of America

# Contents

## Dedication

*To my mother who taught me
while I was young.
To my students who teach me
now that I have grown.*

# Good Morality Is Like Good Cooking and Many Other Things

### Morality Is Like . . .

Over the years of my teaching (and preaching) experience, I have usually sought the use of various analogies in order to get my points across. One parish referred to me as the baseball priest because that summer I used so many baseball examples in my Sunday homilies. In another year my frequent use of the Sunday comics even had the youngsters listening to what I had to say—and they even remembered it afterward! One of the analogies that I have found extremely useful (at least my students liked the approach) was that of good morality is like good cooking. I'd like to develop this one point a little in order to show what can be done with this and other comparisons.

This analogy came to me at an adult discussion group meeting. I was asked to comment on the changes that have taken place in morality over the years. As I reflected upon what it was like back in my grandmother's time and now, the first thought that came to me was how cooking and "morality" have reversed their positions. Back in the late 1800's grandmother cooked everything from scratch and her recipes were in her head. She had no Duncan Hines cake mixes nor Betty Crocker cookbook. She seasoned to taste—lots of oregano for the tomato sauces, not too much sage in the turkey dressing, the right amount of rosemary, thyme and marjoram for the beef roasts. Her meals were a taster's delight! Today we have gone to the other extreme with all kinds of packaged foods and TV dinners, which are usually not what I would consider pleasing to the eye nor to the stomach. Even when following a recipe some cooks are full-fledged literalists. When a teaspoon of cinnamon is called for, they use a knife to scrape it level. They would never add extra spices to what Betty Crocker says; yet, all good cooks know that these special seasonings make the meal. Many have lost much of "this personal flavor" in their way of cooking.

In morality just the opposite has happened. In grandmother's day, life was so much simpler. People lived pretty much the same kind of life; problems were similar; common solutions could often be given. When personal decisions were made that were different from the norm, we did not necessarily know about them, or perhaps even care. Today, though we live in a totally different world. The high speed pressure of living in our modern urban and technological society presents us with a whole new set of problems, each one often different from our neighbor's. We have to make our decisions in situations which have never before existed; they are unique and demand personalized responses. These are not easy to come by, and each of us must become a good cook so that we can put a good "meal" together.

As I reflected more and more on this analogy I came to two conclusions: one was that good morality truly was like good cooking; the other was that this was a non-threatening way to approach morality. We may, like cats, arch our backs when questions in morality are presented, but all of us recognize where we stand in the kitchen—especially our ineptness and our need for help. We can now talk about morality in a much calmer setting.

Throughout the pages of this book use will be made of various analogies. No one comparison will ever do justice to what good Christian morality is all about, and we all know that every comparison has its weak points. It is hoped that the use of examples from different areas (mostly from sports, cooking and music) will enable the reader both to take a fresh look at the various topics discussed and then to come to a clearer and less biased understanding of what good Christian morality is all about.

# Morality

We thus come to what we would call a study of morality, which is that quality of our actions that concerns itself with their human fittingness. Actions are morally good if that is the way a human being should act in order to attain the goal of human living. It respects the nature of the person; it respects the rights of others; it enables us to reach our goal in life. Thus, we need to understand what human beings are, their basic nature, their capabilities and potentialities, their basic goals in life. We must have a solid framework of human values and principles according to which we can make good judgments.

We frequently express these judgements. Parents let their children know what they approve or disapprove of in their children's behavior. Friends share their comments about others. Leaders try to give guidance to the members of their community. In doing so, though, we do run into problems. It seems that in no area of human existence do we humans jealously guard our freedom and privacy as we do in the area of personal morality. It is my life; who can tell me what to do? We grow tense, defensive and even rebellious when someone tries to run our lives for us. We recognize the role and function of parents and all others in authority and we deeply appreciate them. However, we also have an innate feeling that we too know something about life and how it is to be lived by us. In order to defuse this tension and to allow for good communication, we present good morality as being like good cooking.

## Standards in Everything

The fact that morality is going to involve standards according to which we judge the appropriateness of human behavior should not surprise us. They exist in all facets of our human existence, even in such mundane things as people watching.

We are all people watchers, and we are this from a very early age. A small child notices everyone in the store, gets absorbed in what some of them are doing and may even forget about

3

the accompanying adult. Young boys are fascinated by the workers tearing up the streets in the neighborhood. Young adults at the beach survey their surroundings quite thoroughly. The local resident keeps tabs through the front window on all that goes on. Older adults on the park bench reflect on life as they gaze upon the passers-by.

We observe the people and whom they are with, how they are dressed, what they are doing, how they are doing it. As we grow older we start to make comparisons and to pass judgments. Some activities we approve of; others we look down upon and perhaps condemn. Each of us will be coming from slightly different backgrounds and will be making judgments from different vantage points. We also come to realize that different situations will affect how we judge—at work, at school, at home, at play. As we share these with one another we notice the differences, and if we are honest with ourselves we learn that we need to develop a good frame of reference.

We recognize that when we judge we compare what we see with a certain "standard." If we are sincere about it all, we consciously or unconsciously seek to become better acquainted with that standard and all that it entails. We need this if we are to make honest judgments. With little or no taste in clothing, there is little of value that we can say about the way others dress. If we are going to criticize the way others act we need to know more than a little bit about human beings, who and what they are, what their purpose in life is, how they are to go about living. This is what we shall set out to do in the following chapters, but first an illustration.

### Life Is a Large Pizza

Several years ago as a final assignment in a course on Christian ethics I gave my students as one of their options this topic: Good Morality Is Like Good Cooking. As an illustration of how such an analogy can be developed I share with you one of these papers. Here is the one (slightly edited) written by Kathy Riepenhoff.

A good cook learns most of her basic skills from her mother and past failures, and improves by experimenting with, and testing, new recipes. We develop our morality in much the same way. We receive our basic life directions from God. We learn from our past experiences and failures, and we must then keep ourselves open to new ideas and question our moral decisions. Good morality is much like good cooking. Preparing a beautiful meal that makes ourselves and others happy is challenging, but, in the end, fruitful. Developing a mature moral outlook takes just the right combination of ingredients, but once we form that good morality, it points us toward a happy, fruitful and challenging life.

The basic essentials for forming morality are: God, ourselves, and others. These are like salt, sugar and flour—staple groceries that are absolutely necessary for the good cook. We must first see that we are, that we exist. But we can only see ourselves in relation to God and others. God is our Creator who made us as persons, as human beings. He brought us into this world as good people. We have dignity and a destiny. We exist in the nature of freedom, intelligence, feelings and sensations. No one else is exactly like us. We are unique. Human nature has been "put into" all of us, but it develops differently in each person.

The cook must next add other ingredients to bring flavor, spice and creativity to her recipe. She tastes it to test how well they all blend together. For us, freedom, responsibility and values grow to be a part of our basic human nature. We must test these ingredients out to develop just the right blend of them. We experiment to discover the right mixture of values that fit together and complement each other. Just as a cook must alter her recipes to suit the tastes of different people, so we must shift our values to apply them to the unique situations we encounter. This is what we described as a morality of tension. It is a union of our principles and the circumstances involved.

Freedom is one of the most basic gifts given to us. Just as a cook must learn to add exactly the right amount of spices, we must learn to exercise our freedom in the proper degree. It is limited by our physical, emotional and past self. None of our

5

freedoms are absolute. We are free to do as we please, but we can't go around and beat up other people. Our freedom must be developed in the right way. Just as pie isn't complete without ice cream, we can't have freedom without responsibility. We are free to act, but we are then responsible for our actions. We are also responsible for ourselves. God trusts us to be stewards of our bodies and minds. We are free to shape ourselves, and our responsibilities spring from this freedom. We may be free to get drunk, serve others, gossip, help the poor, hurt others, etc., but we are responsible for the outcome of our actions. We must examine them to determine which ones are human, just actions. Would God approve of what we are doing if he were right beside us? We must account for our actions in the end.

A cook strives to improve her skill. She works to make her food even better, always pushing for perfection. We also journey toward God and perfection. We strive to become better, growing to develop good habits and virtues. The seven steps may help us achieve these positive, good actions. We should grow to be mature Christians, but the road to God is a rough, challenging road. We are called to walk in Jesus' footsteps—to undergo sacrifices to bring us one step closer to our Father. We know we can never reach his perfection, but we must work to become the best possible people we can be.

A cook learns her skill from her mother, the advice of others, and her own mistakes. We also learn our ethics from many different sources. When we are younger, laws direct us. This is similar to mom's careful directions when we helped her bake cookies as a child. We follow the laws, but we don't really understand their meaning or purpose. As we get older, we adopt many of our attitudes from our parents and families. We also look to our environment for direction. This may, at times, lead us in the wrong direction because of our society's stress on materialism. Things like TV, movies and magazines paint unrealistic pictures of humans. They set up a false, materialistic standard for us to work toward. But God created us as people who are basically good. The Church, Christ, Scripture, and our community become important in our formation. They help us in the development of our conscience. This dictates our response to a particular moral obligation. Conscience is our whole attitude that makes us aware of the demands of these moral obligations. It involves our basic decision-making process. First, we must have some basic standards and values. Then we must apply these to the situation—seeing and judging it clearly. We can then make a decision and put it into action. But this decision again includes God, Scripture, prayer, community and even our own feelings.

Any cook knows that no matter how hard she scrubs the carrots and potatoes or how carefully she checks the dishes, she can never get every speck of dirt off of them. But she still tries her very best to accomplish cleanliness. We must also realize that no matter how hard we clean ourselves, we can never be totally spotless. We all sin, but we must continue to push forward to the good and clean life. It is important to realize the impossibility of being spotless. If we don't, we will end up discouraged and disappointed. We must see our actual possibilities and set goals for ourselves accordingly. We should see our strengths and weaknesses, and work to be as good as we possibly can.

But even the best cook occasionally produces a flop, and even a good person fails in her journey. She may neglect her friendship with God. Any sin is wrong because it violates our relationship/friendship with God. But we cannot judge unless we have the total picture of the person and the situation involved. Small sins throw us slightly off the track, and it is not too hard to correct our failure and get back on the right path. But when we commit a mortal sin, we are turning around totally—moving in the opposite direction from goodness. Then it becomes much harder to get back on track. But conversion is possible with the help of God and others. We may be enlightened to see the true way and return to God. The sacrament of reconciliation can help us overcome our sins because it forces us to think about where we stand with God. We get advice; we strengthen our own commitment; and God's healing power is focused on us.

Finally, the table is set and the food is ready. The cook can only go ahead with the meal and hope that everything will turn out well. We must also push ahead and live for the present, only hoping that we make decisions that will lead us to a good tomorrow. We come alive with the love of God, which leads us to love others and ourselves. We cannot dwell on problems too much. We must go on living, trusting God to carry us when we come upon rough spots in life. We can only be happy and satisfied when we are living to serve God and others. Life is a continual search for truth. We must always remember that we are only called to do the best that is possible for us. In any situation we can only hope to achieve the most good and least evil that is possible. Life itself is our greatest treasure.

God said, "I have come that you may have life—life to the full." But life is only lived in relation to others; therefore we must live to give life to others by serving them. It is only through service that we ourselves are fulfilled. Because the gift of life is God-given, no human has the right to take it away. We must protect, nurture, and develop the most valuable of God's creations—the life of human persons. Just as a good cook is happy when she produces a good meal, we can be happy when we live a good, moral life. We have all the ingredients—God, others, self, community, church, life, freedom, responsibility and intelligence. It is our duty to grow and learn to blend them into the right mixture.

I think life can be described as a large pizza. God is the dough—the basic part which holds up everything else. A pizza would fall apart without the dough as a base. The sauce represents love, which flows over all of life. Pizza would be dry and lifeless without the sauce. Pepperoni stands for all the people, and the cheese is the stringy tangled web of human relationships which holds people together. Other ingredients like onions, mushrooms, sausage, olives, and peppers are combined differently to add unique flavor to the pizza. Freedom, personality, feelings, responsibilities, looks, and emotions are all ingredients which combine and develop differently in each person to make him or her unique. Finally, the spices and seasonings symbolize humor and laughter which are sprinkled over life to make it taste even better!

*Points for Discussion and Reflection*

1. Are you a moral person? How can you tell?

2. What image of a human being is presented in advertising? TV programs? Movies? Songs? What obligation do we have to see that good images are presented?

3. How does the analogy "Good morality is like good cooking" strike you?

4. Should we all look upon human beings and their actions in exactly the same way? Why or why not?

5. Why are "soaps" watched so much by young adults?

6. Draw your own life-line. Indicate the important dates, events, and people in your life. How has each one of these had an impact on you?

# You Do Not Play Basketball with a Football

In the world of sports there are many games played with a ball, but not with the same kind of ball. There are footballs, basketballs, baseballs, soccerballs, volleyballs, golfballs and even beach balls! Games differ from games; each has its own rules; each has its own court or field of play; each has a different number of participants. When you decide to engage in a particular sport you commit yourself to a definite set of rules; you do not make up your own as you go along. In other words you have to respect the basic nature of the game and play it as it was meant to be played.

The same holds true in the case of the game of life. We need to respect the basic nature of human living. Thus, when we make decisions, or give directions, in regard to good human behavior we need to consider such questions as: Who are we? What is our basic nature? What is our goal in life? With this knowledge we can make more intelligent decisions about what should be done here and now. Reflecting upon the following points should help us arrive at a fuller understanding of who we are as Christians and what is our basic goal in life.

a. We are human beings.
b. We are children of God.
c. By becoming one of us, Jesus Christ tells us a lot about God and ourselves.
d. Our basic calling is to love.
e. This love is triangular.

10

# Human Beings

When we view creation we cannot help but notice that there are basic laws. Everything that exists has a certain nature and acts in accord with that nature. Water runs downhill; smoke rises; fire is hot; sugar is sweet; birds fly; snakes crawl. What about us? Do we have a special nature? How are we to act?

We recognize right away that we are different from all other creatures. Yes, we are subject to the various physical and biological laws of nature but we are much more than a rock, a tree, or a dog. In living we cannot ignore the dictates of these laws; we do not step off the roof of a building and flap our arms to fly! However, we readily see that we can do more than our physical nature allows. We can use our intelligence and various resources and put together a hang-glider or an airplane which will enable us to fly. We have bodies but we also have special human gifts—the ability to think, to make decisions, to carry them out, etc. Our basic actions still have meaning in themselves, but our living is much more complex.

Eating is for nourishment; speaking is for communication; loving is for nurturing and creating. But look at what happens when we add certain circumstances: eating meat on a Friday in Lent (for Catholics); singing in a church rather than the shower; showing love via a gift of candy or gift of myself. These circumstances (what, when, where, how, by what means) add new dimensions to our activity. What is good at one time and place may not be appropriate elsewhere.

Another circumstance (why) can produce even more decisive results. In fact, the reason why we do something may give a very special meaning to what we are doing. Not eating, for instance, could be a number of things—anorexia, dieting, fasting (e.g., skipping a meal and giving the money saved to the starving in Latin America). By speaking I may share with you my own thoughts and feelings or I may be manipulating you to do something for me.

Why did God make us? To know him, to love him, and to

serve him in this life, and to be happy with him in the next. This says a lot about "who" (another circumstance) we are and what is our calling in life and shall be looked at in the next sections.

## Children of God

Who we are in relation to one another is important and will have its own impact upon what we do. Being greeted by a stranger is not the same thing as being greeted by a friend. An insult or a cutting remark from a casual acquaintance never hurts as much as one coming from my spouse or a close friend. Kissing my sister or brother is not the same as kissing someone else's. Who are we in relation to God?

Our Christian heritage tells us that God is not just our Creator; we are not just his servants. Jesus tells us to call God "Father" as a way to manifest the deep personal relationship that exists between us. God created us with a nature that is able to know and love. We are beings who can *freely* enter into love relationships with others. There is no force inside or outside of us that makes us enter into this deep, personal friendship with another. That is why it is something special. Out of all the possible human beings that are, I freely choose *you* to be my friend.

In creating us, God went much further than giving us what our basic nature demanded. In order to enter into a love relationship with God, we had to have a special nature. On the other hand, we had to be able to share in a special way with the Divinity so that we could enter into a personal union with him. We needed a kind of likeness of nature. For instance, you can have a special relationship with an animal that you consider your pet. However, even though we use the expression "man's best friend," dogs cannot enter into the deep, personal relationship with us that we experience with one another. That "likeness of nature" is missing in the dog.

In order to enter into a personal love relationship with God, we need to share in the divine nature. This is what we call "grace," a gift that is freely given and freely accepted—or rejected. By freely accepting it, we can be elevated to a higher existence and we become able to enter freely and personally into a deep love relationship with God. We are his children in a very special way.

## Jesus Christ Says . . .

Actions speak louder than words. By becoming one of us, Jesus Christ, Son of God, become son of Mary, says quite a lot about God and us. We are special. God thinks about us. God loves us. Despite all its imperfections, human nature is good. In a way, by sending his Son among us, God performed a "marriage" between the human nature and the divine nature. His incarnation is a love match. All that God made is good, and to show us both our goodness and our destiny, God united the two natures in the person of Jesus Christ. Reflection upon the mystery of the incarnation should lead us to have a great appreciation for who we are and for what we destined to be, united intimately with God.

Jesus is our teacher. He invites us to come, to follow him. "Yes, come, follow me. In becoming one of you, I am taking upon myself your very own nature so that I can live the life a human being lives. I am the way, the truth and the life. I will show you how you are to live. In my own human existence, I will manifest a good set of values and will show you what life is all about. In all my teachings I will give you solid principles that you are to incorporate into your own existence. I am your brother. I am your teacher who sets out a path for you to follow through the wilderness of human existence. Come, follow me. Walk in my footsteps."

Jesus is our Redeemer. We humans are sinners; we make many mistakes. In our weakness we turn away from God—sometimes far away—and find our pleasure in earthly things. Instead of living as lovers, as real givers, we live as selfish individuals, interested only in self-gratification. As a result we need redemption. We need to be set free from these shackles of sinfulness in order to live the life of love exemplified and taught by Jesus in the New Testament. This redemption Jesus accomplished by coming, taking our sins upon himself and dying for us on the cross. He showed us how much God loves his people.

## Call To Love

God, who is love, invites us to enter into a love relationship with him and with all that is related to him. We are to love God, we are to love ourselves, we are to love our neighbor, we are to love all of God's creation. A consideration of the mysteries of the Trinity and of creation, a glance at God's revelation in both the Old and the New Testaments, a brief overview of Christian history all point out that love is central to our Christian existence. We are all called to love.

Our Christian tradition presents God as Trinity. God is love and love is fruitful. Love gives itself more and more totally the more perfect it is. Thus, we can see the Person we traditionally call "Father," giving self completely to the Second Person whom we have called "Son," a complete revelation of the Father. The Spirit is then the complete revelation of the Father and the Son, knowing and loving each other fully. There are deep, total love relationships between the persons of the Trinity, and we use "love words" when talking about them—Father, Son and Spirit.

Love, too, is at the heart of creation. Love always moves a person to go outside of self, to share what one has and what one is with others. God shares self in that unique way in the Trinity, but that is not enough. This perfect love wants to share itself with others. Just as we share in proportion to what we have and how this can be shared, so too does God. Love moved God to create, to share the perfection of the Godhead in an infinite variety of ways with all of creation and with us, images of God, in a very special way. In creating us unto his own image, God gave us a nature that is able to know, love and enter freely into love relationships. He loved us so much that he sent his only Son both to redeem us from our sins and to teach us how to live.

As God's special creatures, his children, we are called to a life of love. His revelation to us, contained in the Old and New Testaments of our Christian Scriptures, presents love as the

14

basic law of human living. Deuteronomy (6:4–9) has this wonderful passage:

> Hear, O Israel: The Lord our God is one Lord; and you shall love the Lord your God with all your heart, and with all your soul, and with all your might, and these words which I command you this day shall be upon your heart, and you shall teach them diligently to your children, and shall talk of them when you sit in your house; and when you walk by the way and when you lie down and when you rise. And you shall bind them as a sign upon your hand and they shall be as frontlets between your eyes. And you shall write them on the doorposts of your house and on your gates.

It is no wonder then that the Israelites were asked to be faithful to the covenant with the Lord God Yahweh, that Israel was often referred to as the spouse of Yahweh, that sin was frequently called adultery.

The New Testament carries this same teaching a bit further. Jesus came as the One who was to love unto death and who continues to give himself totally in the Eucharist. He invites us all to come, follow him, the greatest lover of all. When giving us the two basic commandments, he repeated the passage from Deuteronomy for the first one (love God with your whole being), and then added: love your neighbor as yourself. All rules regarding human living are contained in these two commandments. Throughout the Gospel accounts we are exhorted to love as Jesus did, to love in deed and truth, to love one another because love unites us to God. St. Paul in his epistles continues the same theme. Love is the fulfillment of the law. Walk in a manner worthy of your calling to be one with Christ, your brother. Everyone is acquainted with his famous description of the excellence of charity in 1 Corinthians 13: the greatest of these is charity!

Our Christian history testifies to our human efforts to respond to this call to love. Love of Christ and this good news about life inspired the early Christians to live such lives of love that it was said of them, "See how they love one another." Love led the apostles, and missionaries throughout the ages, to spread the good news, to share it with others. The spiritual and corporal works of mercy characterize the Church and its various undertakings. The Christian community was carrying out Christ's directive to love and put this into practice via hospitals, schools, hospices, etc. A study of the multitude of religious communities of men and women that sprang up over the centuries is a tremendous testimony to this saying of St. John, "How can we love God, whom we do not see, if we do not love our neighbor whom we do see?" It is love that sees the heart, the values of each human life, and impels people to give so fully of themselves to the service of others.

Yes, God, who is love, invites us all to be members of his kingdom and to enter into a love relationship with him and with all who are members of his kingdom. We are to love God, we are to love ourselves, we are to love our neighbors, we are to love all of God's creation.

## Triangle of Love

True love always keeps in mind the total picture. We love as human beings who have relationships with others. When I love you, I love the "all of you"—your self, your relationship with God, your relationship with other people and with all of creation. That love can be symbolized by a triangle I learned from a former student of mine. When Diana and Jim corresponded, they signed their letters with a triangle. Why? The triangle was a constant reminder to both of them of the three loves in their lives—God, my intended spouse, and myself.

Christ's two commandments include all three loves. Did he not also say, "Whatever you do to these others, my brothers and sisters, you do unto me"? Thus, our love must have a positive impact upon all three. My love of self must aid my love of God and love of neighbor. My love of God should enhance my love of self and neighbor. My love of neighbor should contribute to my love of God and self, and to my neighbor's love of God and self.

When I love you, I love you for all that you are and all that you have—your self, your friends, your God. I want to do all that I can for you and to make everything around you better. I want to improve myself because then I have more to give you. I grow in my relationship with my God, who is also your God. I cannot relate to him nor talk to him without talking about all that I hold dear—that means you. These three loves are so fundamental and so intertwined that I can never truly love one without the other. Just as the fingers on a hand grow in proper proportion, so too do our loves. When I grow in love of God, I become better and have more to offer you. In loving you I stimulate a response in you by which you are naturally moved to respond to my love, and that makes me a better person. You see my relationship with God and are led to a closer bond with him.

Thus, I study not just to get good grades and a high paying job. I devote myself to these pursuits so that I develop the talents within me. These can then be used for the proper service of others, including God. I do not cheat; I do not just get by; I do not spend all my time studying to the neglect of others and God. I strive to be the best possible student I can be right now. Likewise, being a good doctor is not just earning a lot of money and a good reputation. It is using my God-given talents to heal the hurts of others. I serve all and not just those who can pay, or pay well.

I pray; I spend time with God. I can even go to Mass with my date or pray the rosary while driving long distances with my intended spouse. But not all dates take place in church. A mother is at home caring for her sick child; she is not at a prayer meeting. I am attending my 12:00 class instead of the noon Mass. I spend these hours studying for a test rather than reading the Bible and praying that the Spirit will take over at exam time. However, a certain amount of prayer and reflection can calm me down and enable me to study more fruitfully than if I had devoted all the time to study.

I use my money for good purposes; I do not waste it. Having a beer or two might be the best thing for me, but getting drunk is not a proper use of myself, my time, my resources. It hurts my friends. They do not find me a terrific companion when I'm obnoxiously drunk. I tithe to the Church but I do not neglect the needs of my family. Instead of buying another Porsche to put into my garage, I give the money to a scholarship fund for needy students.

I never forget that I am a member of God's kingdom and that all I say and do will help—or hinder—the total establishment of God's kingdom throughout the world. God's loving kindness is to permeate the entire universe, and all creation is to mirror the goodness of the Lord.

Thus, in making our decisions, we need to consider our obligations to the triangle and how this action will affect each of the three. We strive to make those decisions that best enhance the triangle. St. Augustine's saying—Love, and then do what you will—is true.

Years ago, a friend told me that he and his wife never felt more in love with each other than when they were side by side at the Eucharistic table. I passed this along to my students, and later a few of them came back and said, "It's true." Other experiences in my life and in the lives of my friends continue to bear witness to this triangle of love.

We must love all three aspects and their totality, i.e., in themselves and in their relationship with the other two. We cannot ignore any one part. Love is total or it is not completely true love. That is why St. John calls certain people "liars." How can you love God whom you do not see, if you do not even love your neighbor whom you do see? We need to love all God's children; we need to love all our brothers and sisters, no matter who or where they are. This *social* dimension to our love life is one that tends to be most neglected. More on this later.

## Summary

How to summarize all this? It is quite evident that a human being, especially from a Christian perspective, is very complicated. However, the following five terms do give us a good description of a human person that will serve our purposes: individual, incarnate, religious, social, perfectible/historical.

As *individuals*, we are free and responsible persons who can know and love. We recognize values, make judgments and are personally responsible for what we do. We can give the free response of a friend, conveying all the uniqueness of who I now am and of who I am ever becoming.

We are *incarnate* persons, i.e., we are body-soul. Because of this, there are things we can and cannot do. We have the challenge of putting the two (body and soul) together into a disciplined whole. We are not born mature but we can develop into integrated persons. We can never forget that we have bodies that have needs and limitations. Brother Ass, as St. Francis called his body, needs to be properly cared for. After all, he does take us wherever we want to go and helps us do what we want to do. Likewise, our spiritual side lets us know that we are more than bodies and that more is expected of us than of animals.

We are *religious*, i.e., related to God. We are creatures with a special nature that can know and love this God freely and completely. We are capable of sharing the divine nature by grace. We can truly be called children of God and have that personal relationship with God that children have with their father and mother.

We are *social* beings. While it is true that we are individuals, we would not be what we are without others. To some extent, we are products of society and we help to create society. We live with others, we need others, we grow and develop through others, we are influenced by others, we have an impact upon others. Further, our call to love God is a call to love as a whole, not as a bunch of isolated beings. We all have the same goal and are called to the same intimate relationship, but we are to do this as unique individuals so closely related to one another that we move as "one." This social aspect of all we do needs constant and serious attention.

We are *perfectible* beings. We are historically conditioned and situated. We live in a definite time in history and we are also at a specific point on our own time-line with a unique history of our own. We are pilgrims, moving on toward the fullness of our own lifespan. We are also human, imperfect beings, capable of making mistakes. We are sinners; we often do what we ought not to do. But as pilgrims, progressing along the way toward the attainment of our ideal, we are able to rise above sinfulness and grow into a better love relationship with God. Thus, even though we are wounded, we are perfectible. We can grow into real lovers of God.

In sum, we human beings are special. We have been given a nature endowed with very special gifts and destined for a very special goal in life—a personal union with God as members of his kingdom. Thus, when we consider what is morally good for us, we have to make our decision in the light of who we are in relation to God, to ourselves and to the world around us. We are stewards who are one day to render an account of our stewardship over ourselves, over our sisters and brothers, and over all God's creation. We are all part and parcel of his kingdom. We are to live the game of life, created by someone far above us, who has already set down the basic rules and goals!

*Points for Discussion and Reflection*

1. What does being in the state of grace mean to you?
2. Why should we be more familiar with the Bible, especially the New Testament?
3. What can we learn by keeping a journal of our daily lives?
4. Is it true that in love, an invitation is more binding than an order, coolness is more wounding than betrayal?
5. Give several examples of your own to show how circumstances can change the nature and/or meaning of an action.
6. What does "following Christ" mean to you?
7. Does our society today promote good Christian living? Give examples from your own life to help prove your point.
8. If there are three loves (God, neighbor, self) why did Jesus only give us two commandments, to love God and to love our neighbor?

# Information, Please!

All of us, at one time or another, seek information and are only too glad that there are resources to consult. We go to dictionaries for definitions and spellings, to phone books for telephone numbers, to maps for directions in traveling, to cookbooks for recipes and suggestions on how to prepare a meal. When shopping in a large supermarket for a seldom-used object, most of us usually find it time-saving to ask a store employee where to find it. States have tourist information centers; large buildings have office directories; and there is always the 555-1212 number to call. We often talk to a classmate to check on a class assignment. We ask a friend for directions on how to get to his house. We are grateful to have as a lab partner someone who really knows what is going on in the course. This need for information that we do not have is with us all our lives, and intelligent people never hesitate to ask for help. There is always a place in our lives for someone who knows more about life than we do.

## Human Living

In our own lives as human beings we are faced with putting good human acts together into a healthy and satisfying human life moving us toward the attainment of our goal of existence. This is not an easy task. We have so many parts, each competing for attention and satisfaction—our minds, our hearts, our bellies, our souls. There are many ways to satisfy our cravings— some good, and some bad. How are we to recognize what is good for us? Further, there is sin. Lots of people around us are all for sin and want to convert us to sinful ways of living. In addition, we humans are creatures who take a very long time to mature— longer than almost all other creatures. This personal maturation—not just physical—does not come with experience. Only perfect practice makes perfect. Even if we could do it all by ourselves, look at how long a trial and error process would take.

## Authority

Thus, in our moral lives we do need teachers—our parents, our teachers, our religious leaders. We need to be taught from the cradle to the grave—at mom's knee, in school, as mature people. Learning goes on and on. We need to be taught by teachers who have experienced life, who have insights into what true human living is all about and who can communicate with us. We need to be taught the basic values in life (what is important and why), the basic goodness and badness of certain actions, what is involved in making decisions, what it means to be responsible.

Authority is an essential part of our lives. People in authority are there primarily to serve by helping us to grow, to mature, to become the persons we are capable of being. They point out dangers and pitfalls; they give us directions; they share their insights. They endeavor to help us avoid mistakes and grow up more graciously. Theirs is a great responsibility. We on our part are to recognize their role and to accept the teaching and the guidance they offer us. We cannot just take what we want and pitch the rest. Yes, we can and should ask questions and seek a deeper understanding of what is going on. But like good apprentices in the kitchen or as a rookie on a team we do this respectfully and sincerely as a means to grow into something better.

## Law

Furthermore we need laws and principles spelled out for us like numbers in a phone book or recipes in a cookbook. We need help when we are young, ignorant, inexperienced; and later when we are more mature we need to be able to double-check our positions against those of the more experienced. Laws are there to direct us on our way. They instruct us, especially when we are driving down an unfamiliar road. We appreciate "bump," "sharp curve," "dangerous intersection," "truck entrance." We are made aware of items we need to know in order to drive safely and responsibly. Laws, or more correctly these formulations of laws, reflect reality; they do not create it. Saying that falling objects accelerate 32.2 feet per second squared just reflects what happens; it does not cause it. All good laws mirror what is already there.

Since laws are there to guide and help us live humanly, they are defined as ordinances of reason for the common good, made by proper authority and promulgated. It is our reason that sees reality as it is, that sees the truth of things, that is able to see what means should be used in order to attain the end in view. Laws and regulations are concerned with the good of the overall group. Only proper authority, i.e., qualified people in charge of a community, can make laws for its people. The state of Indiana does not make laws for the citizens of Ohio. Teachers of young students know the answer to "Mr. Jones and Mrs. Smith let me do this." If my parents give me an 11:00 P.M. curfew, I cannot use Tim's curfew of midnight and expect nothing to be said. Finally, all laws and rules need to be made known. We cannot be held responsible for breaking laws that no one knew about.

The basic purpose of laws and regulations is to help us grow up with a minimum of mistakes. "Wet paint," "out of order," "beware of dog," can be useful signs. Laws facilitate us in our development as human beings. They point out the right way to go. Telephone books take the place of random dialing. Street signs and road maps are a blessing to drivers from out of state. Cookbooks save us a lot of grief in the kitchen. Laws free us from the shackles of selfishness and ignorance; they enable us to live the human life in all its fullness. For some strange reason—probably because of a lack of proper understanding—laws have tended to produce legalism and minimal morality, rather than a strong thrust toward the ideal.

In human living, too, laws are necessary. We learn; we are not born mature. We have to grow up so we can act our age. We not only learn to counteract ignorance (i.e., not knowing) but we also have to correct the misinformation that we pick up along the way, often because we have not heard the whole story. Learning is not always easy. We are not all "students" by nature; we may be lazy and easily distracted. Learning on our own would take a long time, and we would often end up being products of unskilled labor. Further, we are sinners; we do not always do what is right; we may develop wrong patterns of behavior. We need to be told we are going the wrong way on a one way street. The social implications of all that we are and all that we do are both numerous and complicated. We just cannot do it all on our own. When you add to this the fact that we are called to be followers of Christ and special friends of God throughout our entire existence, it is easy to see that having laws and signposts are very good things.

## Natural Law

But what about our basic nature? Did not God give us something special? Are we not personally able to see who we are, what our goals are, how we are to get there? Are we not able to act on our own?

The theoretical answer is "yes." This is basically what we mean by "natural law." We human beings have a certain nature; there are basic human inclinations; there are basic moral principles guiding the way we should live. We have the capacity whereby we can, through insight into our human nature and into the goals of human existence, see how we should conduct ourselves in order to act in accord with our own nature and in line with our goals.

We can recognize our basic inclinations and their primary implications. Our three basic tendencies are to preserve self, to reproduce self and to be a self. Self-preservation is tied in with questions of health, self-defense, medical operations, prolongation of life, suicide, etc. Self-reproduction involves marriage, education of children, proper use of sexual powers, right to family wage, etc. Being a human person includes learning, living peacefully with others and acknowledging our Creator. General moral principles that we can come up with would include directions like the following:

24

1. Do good and avoid evil.
2. Strive to be your full self.
3. Learn.
4. Take good care of your bodily life.
5. Use "irrational" creatures properly, as stewards, not absolute owners of them.
6. Make your contributions to society.
7. Treat all your sisters and brothers as equals.

Much of this, and maybe all of it, we could discover and then act accordingly. However, as stated above, there are at least three other factors that must be considered and which make the function of law and authority necessary. First, we humans are not perfect. We make a lot of mistakes. We can too easily be distracted and led astray. Second, life is complicated. It always was, and today seems even more so. It is almost impossible for each of us to know the social interrelatedness of all we do. Just what are all the implications of the above seven principles? Third, our Christian heritage tells us that we are called to an intimate life of friendship with God. How could we know this if it had not been revealed?

### Dissent

Wherever you have law and authority, you will also find challenges. From birth on we learn by questioning and testing. We do this with authority even when we are babies; as teenagers we often seem rebellious as we challenge the status quo; as adults we are more willing to accept authority in general (they can set down the general guidelines) but proper applications must be made to our own situations. No one knows us as we ourselves do. Times change; current laws do not clearly address the problems we are experiencing in our lives right now. What is to be done? This question of dissent (challenging authority, questioning the fullness of the truth expressed) is a fundamental part of human living. At times it can be a duty as well as a right. Such challenges, as well as the healthy dialogue that should result, can lead to greater insights into the moral demands of the current situation. This should then produce a clarification in the formulation of the law.

There are problems, however. This process is a time-consuming one. In our age of "instantness" we like to see the changes take place now. Further, each case is different. How can the basic moral guidelines be expressed so that they truly cover all situations and do not lead to an infinity of exceptions? Again, we are called to be Christians, followers of Christ. Just what does this mean? Can challenges be addressed to us? Can a little of the heroic be asked of us now and then? Is there a difference in acting biologically, humanly and Christianly?

From our own experiences we can know that some changes in the law or in the stand taken by authority need to be made. These "gut feelings" are often very correct. The problem with them is two-fold: just what changes should be made and what do we do until they are made. Many young people think their parents are too strict, not very understanding, too unrealistic in their curfews, etc. At times they may be right, but not always. A widower friend of mine shared the following experience with me. When his children were growing up, they were always home at reasonable hours. When they started college, things changed. Midnight was early. They would come in at 2 A.M., 3 A.M., and even 4 A.M. Dad could never understand why nor could he get from them any "reasonable" explanation of why anyone would stay out that late. Sometime after his wife died, he began to do a little socializing himself. He still had one college-age daughter living at home. One night he did not get in until 4:30 A.M. Awaiting him on the house bulletin board (the refrigerator) was this message in large print: NOW YOU KNOW!

What is to be done about the problems, whether they be in the family, the school, the community, or the Church? How soon can we find out what change should be made? There is no set time for this. Rarely does it occur overnight; most often it takes a long time. Change in any community's rules seems to take longer in proportion to the size of the group. Coming up with an answer that makes sense to a variety of peoples and cultures is no easy task. Good sauce is a long time simmering on the stove. Good recipes are tried and tested many times before they appear in a cookbook. It is rare, very rare, for a teenage athlete to make a successful jump to the big leagues.

What do I do in the meantime—run away from home, drop out of school, leave the Church, go to another country? These are all possible solutions but they do not solve the problem at hand; and since they cut me off from the group, I can have no impact upon authority. They might just say "good riddance to bad rubbish." Usually it's better to stay and work toward the changes needed. We can continue to raise questions, contribute our insights, respond intelligently to the thoughts of others. The dialectic between us should lead to a greater understanding of what is to be done and how to go about doing it.

Am I still to follow my conscience in all this? Yes, in general we must always follow our conscience when it is certain and true. But that is the problem. We at times may overestimate our personal competence and may be blind to the real reasons we have for seeking the change. Furthermore, a very important concern should be our own growth and development as members of this faith community. Just how acquainted am I with the basic commitments (and reasons for them) of this community? How well do I know Jesus, the founder and basic teacher? Do we share a deep intimate relationship? Thus, we may not always be completely right in our position and strong questions may be raised in its regard. That is why we need to be willing to consult others and above all to reflect prayerfully on all aspects of the situation with a complete openness to following the Spirit. There may be no set book solution to many of our problems, but an answer can be found through proper consultation.

*Points for Discussion and Reflection*

1. Does law destroy one's freedom? Explain.
2. What is the role of rules in the education and formation of the young?

3. Should human law direct or reflect social conditions? Is law a legitimate instrument of social reform?
4. They govern best who govern least.
5. Discuss: censorship, movie critics, book reviews, food and drug laws, food editor of a newspaper.
6. Can Scripture be called a cookbook for human living?
7. From daily newspapers or from your daily life select examples that show how laws are a help to us.

# From Slugs to Hugs                                          **4**

In recent decades we have moved to a more positive understanding of human nature and its foibles. Years ago "spare the rod and spoil the child" was in vogue. Now we are more inclined to hug than to slug. This is true in all walks of life; mistakes are made—in sports, in typing, in driving, in playing a musical instrument. We need to have our errors pointed out to us in a clear and firm manner, but most of us seem to grow better with a pat on the back and a word of encouragement than a kick in the pants. But like everything else, "hugs not slugs" will have its drawbacks. We do need sufficient discipline and correction in our lives so that we do not become lazy and not see the awfulness that sin really is, and end up tolerating it as a part of our lives. We may need a stern taskmaster—a demanding coach, a strict director of music to help us toe the mark and become what we are capable of being. We certainly do need to take a good look at sin and how to eliminate it from our lives.

## What Is Sin?

There is sin in our lives. We do make mistakes; we do the wrong thing. Lying is wrong. So are hurting others, drunkenness, adultery, cheating, laziness. But what makes a sin a sin? There are different ways of looking at sin and sinfulness. By considering several of them we can come up with a better understanding of what sin is all about.

Our sins are a misuse of God's gifts to us. We use the scissors to cut the tablecloth, the pen to write on the wall, the knife to scratch the woodwork. Our tongue is for proper communication, not for lies, profanity, obscenity, detraction, disrespect. Sexuality is a tremendous gift for love and for life, not for lust or playing around. Material things (alcohol, food, the automobile) are for our use, not abuse. When we do not use things in the way that is consistent with their basic nature and purpose, then we sin.

Sin is an unloving way to act. No matter if it is just a mere oversight or a slap in the face, this is not the way to show love and care for another. We are called to love and to love all. Love has the best interests of the others at heart. We care about them; we want them to be the best and to have the best. We help them grow. We avoid what can hurt them, upset them or hinder their growth and development. We do for them what enables them to enjoy life more and what facilitates their growth into fuller persons. Read again St. Paul's description of love in 1 Corinthians 13. With this in mind it is a lot easier to understand sin as an unloving way to act.

At times we describe sin as "saying no to God." This is true, but unless we look deep beneath the surface we miss the point. Do you want to go to the ball game with me? NO. How about a walk in the park? NO. Would you like to see a movie? NO. These "no's" do not show what sin is. "No" becomes a sin when we refuse to love, to share our lives with those who love us so deeply—as our lover, our spouse, our God. I take my stand against God who says that whoever is not with him is against him. Sin is not just a simple one-word response; it is a stance taken by the entire person.

Further, sin is a terrible pollution of our human environment; it is never just one beer can tossed by the roadside. Instead of doing our part (like the trees and grass and their natural function of cleaning the air of pollutants and returning oxygen), we belch forth foul smelling gases that gradually destroy what is fresh and clean.

## Distinction of Sins

In the late Middle Ages, we Christians got the idea of quantifying sins, of categorizing them, of ranking them. This stayed with us to the present century. We made the distinction between sins that were mortal (death dealing) and those that were venial (bad, but not producing death). For sins to be mortal we had to know what we were doing, we had to fully consent and they had to be "big." We rated as biggies such things as murder, fornication, masturbation, drunkenness, missing Mass on Sunday. Venial sins were little things like telling lies, fighting with friends, stealing small amounts. Some things like missing morning and night prayers were usually not sins at all though we always confessed them as part of our list of wrongdoings.

As we became more interested in the total person, such distinctions became less important, as did the counting of the number of times we did them. We did not deny that some misdeeds are more serious than others, but we were more concerned with our sinfulness than with our sinful deeds. Thus, in reality, maybe there should be no distinction of sins. In love, all sins are wrong. I just do not go up to someone I love and say this is only a little hurt and then punch him in the nose. About the only distinction that we might want to make would be between sins or actions unbecoming to a Christian in this faith community and sins that destroy my relationship with this community. In the latter case, I have been expelled from the group or I have cut myself off from them by my sins and I need to seek reinstatement. All else should be treated as something wrong, contrary to the way a real lover acts, but we do not give undue emphasis to these bad habits. We do not ignore them, but concentrate on the positive side of our lives, the inculcation of good habits. Plant flowers! A positive approach to good Christian living would do more good than spending a lot of time pulling weeds. If all we do is pull weeds, what is left? A patch of mud. When we plant flowers, there is less room for weeds to grow, and we are encouraged to pull the weeds because they interfere with the beauty of the flowers. Remember the song lyric, "Accentuate the positive, eliminate the negative, and don't mess around with Mr. In-Between."

## Sense of Sin

By acting in this way we may help restore a sense of sin to the world in which we live. We have lost the sense of sin. Just look around. There are two very evident indications of this. First, there is a very high tolerance for sinful deeds. People cheat and do not even bat an eye. The language we hear around us does not faze us; it becomes a part of us. We do not raise our objections to the excessive violence and sex on TV. The entire pornography industry is an accepted way of life. Drunkenness on a college campus is no big deal. Discrimination exists in so many places that we do not recognize it. Wherever we go, we live in a world where sinful behavior is highly tolerated and accepted as a way of life. Second, there is the absence of an atmosphere of community spirit which supports good Christian living. At times such behavior is mocked and ridiculed rather than praised and supported. People have lost the sense of sin. We are not sensitive to its presence around us. We have been so accustomed to living in the midst of sin that it is readily accepted as part of our way of living. Maybe an increase of flowers, some paint, some well-kept yards would all help to beautify the surroundings and point out most clearly that certain things are out of place in this neighborhood.

## Conversion

One day, in the comic strip "For Better Or For Worse," little Michael was having a crummy day and his mother had to put up with it all. Finally, at the end of this hectic day she puts the strongly resisting Mike to bed and then starts to leave the room. "Mom, aren't you even going to hug me goodnight?" "To tell you the truth, Mike, when you act like this I just don't feel like hugging you at all." "But Mom, that's when I need it the most!"

Mike was struggling with life. Being good is not always easy. Christ did not promise us a rose garden. We are human and at times things get the better of us. That is why conversion is part of all our lives. As we grow, we daily have to repent of yesterday's mistakes. We have to take ourselves as we are today and commit this person to a greater love of God, of neighbor and of self. To do this, we need the healing power of love in our lives. Hugs, not slugs.

This call to conversion is nothing new. It is basic to Christianity. When Christ began his public ministry it was with "Repent, convert, the kingdom of God is at hand." Change your hearts, mend your ways. The time is now. Christ, who was to reveal to us what human living was all about, was here. We were to listen to what he had to say and then go and live the message he brought us. Christ recognized that we are sinners, but he saw our potential and knew what we could become. In his treatment of sinners open to grace, Christ always was positive, encouraging, supportive, but at the same time demanding and challenging. The only ones he had trouble with were the hard of heart who closed their minds and hearts to what he had to say.

Our conversion starts with enlightenment. We see in a clearer light who we are in relation to others and to ourselves. We see how our actions affect others as well as ourselves. We see how our past behavior fits in (or does not fit in) with what we are called to be. We see how we were not acting as Christians, how we were not measuring up to Christ's call to follow him. Recognizing all this, we repent. We regret that we were acting in such an un-Christian way. We put it away from us; we reject it as our way of living. Only then can we commit ourselves to Christ's values. We cannot serve two masters. We have to reject the other if we are to serve Christ and live according to his teachings.

For a Christian this act of conversion is nothing other than a true act of faith whereby we accept Christ as our Lord and Savior and commit ourselves unreservedly to him. This does not always include, as it did for St. Paul, getting knocked off a horse, but the results are much the same. I change my ways. I accept Christ's attitudes, his values, his approach to living. I give up those that are worldly and/or un-Christian, and put on the Lord Jesus and his ways of acting—loving, caring, unselfish, totally dedicated to one's mission in life. Deliberate sin and tolerated sin are no longer acceptable. I put them behind me and concentrate on planting as many flowers as I can.

## Sacrament of Reconciliation

We Christians are human. We need to grow and develop. Even without mistakes, we have a lot of growing to do. When we were children we thought and acted as children. When we were adolescents, we thought and acted as such. As adults we are to think and act as adults. Our sinning not only complicates this, but it also points out our weakness and our need for help. "Mom, that's when I need the hug the most."

It is from this perspective that the ecclesial dimension of conversion can be properly understood. The Church was always concerned with the growth of its members into the fullness of faith and Christian living. Each culture, each era brought along its own challenges. The Christian message had to be lived in all its fullness, but not necessarily in the same way. Throughout history the Church has recognized the humanness of its members and has dealt with their mistakes usually in a positive way. Their conversion had to be celebrated, and this ecclesial act of reconciliation or celebration of conversion was adapted to fit the needs of the time. The recent external changes in the sacrament of reconciliation bring this out. The basics are always there— sin, conversion, reconciliation. How these are put together and expressed ritually is another matter. The Church continues Christ's work, and he did forgive sinners their misdeeds. The Church and its people should always be like the forgiving parent, welcoming the prodigal back home. A hug does not mean: go and do it again. Rather it is a way of saying: yes, we both know what you did was wrong, but we still love you for what you really are and we know with our help you can grow into something you and we will both be proud of.

It is true that the sacrament of reconciliation is absolutely necessary only when one has broken with the community either by running away or by having been kicked out. Then the person must be reconciled with the community. However, this does not mean that the sacrament should be used only under such circumstances. It is closely associated with the work of conversion, a work that goes on daily as we grow into being someone better today than we were yesterday. At times this conversion is much more meaningful and beneficial when celebrated in my community. The sacrament requires that the person take a good look at self in order to see just how well he/she has been living up to the Christian challenge to love God, neighbor and self. Regular reception keeps us on our toes, so to speak, and does not allow contentment with mediocrity to set in. The sacrament constantly rekindles our commitment to the Christian way of life. We reject sin; we accept Christ. It furthermore gives us the opportunity to profit from the support of another who happens to be qualified in the matters at hand. An exchange between two people seeking a greater understanding of the truth should produce a greater good. All sacraments are encounters with God and increase our sharing in God's life (grace) each in its own way. The sacrament of reconciliation brings to bear God's loving hugs when and where we need them most.

## Points for Discussion and Reflection

1. Discuss examples of "social sins," i.e., those with broad social implications, that abound today. Cf. the daily newspapers and TV programs for examples.
2. Has our local community lost the sense of sin? How?
3. Sin is to want to be not more human, but less human.
4. Where charity unifies, self-love divides. How is this true in sin?
5. What would be a good celebration of someone's conversion? Spell it out.
6. Only those individuals who have a deep sense of what a commitment is can really understand "sin" and why reconciliation is necessary.
7. Confession is a peak moment in a total process of conversion.

# A Tuba Is Not a Flute

You do not have to be very knowledgeable about music to recognize that a tuba is not a flute and vice versa. Each musical instrument is unique and produces its own particular musical sound. To use the instruments properly the special character of each one has to be recognized and respected. Here, as in so many other areas, the individual is unique and has to be used according to its own specific nature. If you look at the field of individual sports, such as tennis or figure-skating, the same thing is true. Each person is unique, has his/her own specific talents and limitations. In order to be a success one has to "play within one's own limits" and do well what one is capable of doing.

## Be Yourself

Christian morality likewise respects the individual. We are all asked to be ourselves, and this is not a simple task amidst all the pressures we experience as we grow into adulthood and afterward. Parental pressure, peer pressure, societal pressure all push us into definite modes of being and behaving. The way we dress, the way we talk, the way we act are all influenced by those around us. It is not always easy to go our own way when the crowd pushes us in the other direction.

However, this directive to be a person does not mean "do as you please." It does mean we should develop our own unique personality and live the Christian life in our own specific calling, using our own talents, following our formed conscience. We are encouraged to be our own unique selves, pursuing the fullness of the Christian ideal, each in one's own way. We are led to accept the fact that each one of us is something special.

## Be Unique Originals

Actually our calling is to be a unique original. Each of us has his or her own special personality. We may look alike; we may do similar things; but we are not the same. No one else is like me; I am special. As I accept my specialness and grow into adulthood, my actions, flowing from my being, will take on a distinctive flavor. Although we are all members of God's kingdom and work toward its full realization on this earth, I am special. No one else can do what I can do; no one else can contribute what I can give. I am not worried about being like John or like Mary; I want to be "me."

But what does this mean? Christian teaching exhorts us toward the realization of the highest degree of religious and moral conduct. Be perfect as your Father in heaven is perfect. Come, follow me and be another Christ—but in your own unique way. No cheap imitations; personalize it. External conformity is not the key here; rather, in our following Christ, we are to put on his mysteries, i.e., his basic attitudes, and fit them into our way of life. We may not be physically nailed to a cross, but we do have to die to some things in this world. We are told that we shall render an account for every idle word. We must love our enemies and bear wrongs patiently. We must be pure of heart. Even looks and glances can be wrong.

This will often be very demanding but we have been forewarned that followers of Jesus must be willing to undergo every sacrifice for the sake of witnessing the good news to all peoples. Put your hand to the plow and don't look back. If your eye scandalizes you, pluck it out. Love unto death. Do not put your love for brother, mother, spouse above your love for God.

We humans endure many things for the sake of an earthly goal. Look at professional football players grunting and groaning during those first weeks of camp in July. Some might nominate the coaching staffs for awards as sadists of the year. Look, too, at the teenage swimmers who not only give up ice cream sodas and a social life, but even get up in the middle of the night in order to attend swimming practice at 6:00 A.M. To get our bodies into shape we need to diet and exercise. It is not surprising that the same is true when it comes to getting ourselves fully in shape. We are composite beings (body, mind, heart, will) with various needs and tendencies. To harness all our energies, to take care of all our needs, to integrate all our powers we need discipline. This is what it takes to attain control over our senses, our muscles, our emotions, our imagination, our intellect, our will. Getting one member of a drill team to perform a routine correctly is one thing; getting the entire group to do the same in unison is quite a different story. Growing up and becoming a real self is no easy task.

### God's Will

But does being myself fit in with doing God's will? After all, we Christians are asked to conform our will to God's. Look at what Scripture tells us. Christ taught us to pray, "Thy will be done." In the garden he himself prayed, "Not my will but yours be done." Mary at Nazareth replied "Fiat" (your will be done). When we are told that only by complete surrender to God (thy will be done) can we truly live, we find it a hard saying. In the Gospels there are various instances of people who walked away because Jesus asked for too much.

Perhaps our problem is that we tend to absolutize doing God's will, i.e., we think that God has a set program we are to follow in exact detail or we are not doing his will. He does not treat us as computerized robots, inserting a program and pushing a button. Actually, God's will for all creatures is for them to do their own thing, i.e., to act according to your nature. Be human beings. Make decisions but make them rationally. The will of God for me right now is to get up, get dressed, eat and go to my 9:00 class. How I shower, what soap I use, what clothes I wear, what I eat for breakfast, are all incidental. Act according to your total nature so that you can move toward your true goal in life—that's God's will.

## The Real Me

The parable of the talents aptly illustrates what we are discussing. I have been given certain number of talents (10-5-1). I am to use all the ones I have received, develop them and return the final product to the Lord when I come to the end of my life and present myself for admission into the next. I am to be my full self, not a carbon copy of someone else. This is the challenge—to create the real me.

To do this, I must first both know and understand myself. Did you ever stop to think what this entails? My personality, temperament, capacities (physical, psychological, spiritual), talents, strengths, weaknesses, past history, experiences, maturation, current relationships, commitments, goals—and the list could go on. Then I have to take this self, organize it, discipline it. I have to attain control over my faculties and powers so that I can use each one properly. I must know where to go and how to get there. I must know when to go and when to stop. In sum, I must be able to use myself and all that is "me" in the right way. I am not worried about how I compare to some other person. Instead, I must work at developing the best possible me that can exist. This is creative and challenging; it can be measured only by what I can possibly be. That is why we refer to being unique originals rather than cheap imitations. There can be only one real me. It is my responsibility to "create" it. Remember, a good chef can take the most basic ingredients and turn out an excellent meal. A good athlete takes his basic physical attributes and by dint of hard and persistent effort becomes a hall-of-famer.

### Points for Discussion and Reflection

1. Who am I? Write this out.
2. Why is a saint the only "real" human being?
3. Why are good works necessary for us to attain happiness?
4. Can we really be Christian in this modern world? How?
5. Is being "holy" the same thing as being "whole"?

In any group performance putting it all together is the important thing. There are many individuals in the group, each with his/her own special talents and limitations. Having all recognize their particular role to play, having them see what this part contributes to the success of the group, and getting all to produce according to their own specific talents is a major task both for the director and for each member of the group. It takes a lot of hard work. However, the end result is a thing of beauty and a pleasure to behold, e.g., the performance of a drill team, a band or choir concert. In the field of sports this is what championship teams are made of.

## Social Dimension of Human Living

In our human living we are not always conscious of this social dimension of our actions and the impact we have on others. We do not stop to think about this (although we should) before we make our decisions. We Americans in our rugged individualism have concentrated very much on the self. We have always been told that "you can do it." This is the land of opportunity. By dint of hard work you can rise to the heights. Too often our struggle for economic improvement has led us to neglect others. Not only do we overlook their needs, but we even trample them underfoot as we struggle upward. Too often it is everyone for himself.

Although we may not always take time out to consider the relationships we have with others, we cannot avoid having an impact upon them. Whatever we do has its effect, positively or negatively, directly in itself or by example. A pleasant smile, hard work, neatness in what one does never goes unnoticed. Smoking in a crowded room, playing my stereo at peak volume, spilling toxic wastes all have their negative effects. We unconsciously pick up the language used by those around us and can be shocked by the vocabulary we start to use. Children mimic their parents and do what they see their moms and dads doing. My business competitors follow these practices and so do I. I want to survive too. If some of the practices are a little shady, so what!

## The Little Things We Do Have an Impact

Some of the biggest surprises that come our way are those that happen because of what we are. We do not even realize the influence our ordinary daily living and acting has on others. A colleague of mine was most pleasantly shocked upon receiving the following note of appreciation from another colleague:

". . . I'd like to thank you for all the help and guidance which you have provided me over the past several years. Knowing you has made me a more careful, caring teacher. Knowing you has made me a kinder friend and better listener. Knowing you has made me a more loving and appreciative parent and spouse. Knowing you has made me a more perceptive thinker. Knowing you has made me a better Christian and a more compassionate feminist, a more aware leader. I truly appreciate you and am grateful for your time and concern. I look forward to its continuation. I'm really glad you are here."

A priest friend received this note from a former student who was describing her wedding: "Whether you realize it or not, you played a big part in the ceremony. Because of all your guidance, I was able to let go of so many years of anger, and get the most out of the sacrament. It was truly the most joy-filled day in my life, and I really felt God's presence. When we presented a bouquet at the shrine of the Blessed Mother, I told her to bless you for 'bringing me back home.' "

With a little more thoughtfulness, each of us could do so much more. We need to look beyond ourselves. A mother of nine had to be aware of what she was doing when she made this strange request for a birthday present: "Each year on my birthday I want each of you to select a person, preferably a woman, who has been influential in your life and give her a rose as a sign of appreciation." What a beautiful birthday gift and how far-reaching! The stories that each child tells when sharing the experience with mom must be great events. A group of students I know began a group called "Fuzzies" after the folk fable by Richard Lessor. Their pledge read: "I am a Fuzzy. I pledge myself to make my little corner of the world a better place in which to live. By giving of myself to others through a Fuzzy a day, I will let God's light shine through to others." A Fuzzy a day evidently refers to what we once called a good deed. These were people who believed you would accomplish more good by actively doing something rather than by bitching. The old Christopher movement saying, "It's better to light a candle than curse the darkness," is another way of putting it.

## Why?

Why is there a social dimension to everything we do? First, by our very nature we are social beings. We influence others and are influenced by them because that is the way our nature works. We are contributing to our community good things or bad. Even when doing nothing, we would be parasites, living off others, and not doing what we could for the good of all. Further, we are all one family of God. We all form one body of Christ. When one hurts, we all hurt. When one rejoices, we all rejoice. As human beings we are given stewardship over the world and all that is in it. Our stewardship includes all our brothers and sisters no matter who or where they are. We are one day to render an account of our stewardship. What you did to others you did unto me, says the Lord. Both our human and our Christian dimension tells us to be other-centered, not self-centered. In fact this is the best way to really love oneself.

## Direct Action Is Necessary

Not only is there a social side to all we do, but at times in our actions we must choose those options which are decidedly social in nature and in intent. Some challenges that come our Christian way demand that we take actions that will raise the consciousness of society in regard to the problem that exists. In seeking solutions, at times, we need to face the problem head-on. If we don't we become part of the problem.

It woud be nice if by being Fuzzies we could convert the entire world to loving and caring for each other. The real world tells us that this will not happen overnight. Yes, we should continue to be Fuzzies, but in certain instances some of us, or even many of us, must take direct action. Examples of this would be the civil disobedience of Martin Luther King, the Vietnamese protests of the 1960's and 1970's, and the nuclear war protests of the 1980's. Withholding taxes, trespassing, picketing, boycotting are all steps taken to bring attention to problem areas and to challenge all of us to do something about them. World hunger, exploitation of third world countries, and American policies in Latin America are just a few of the areas that need attention today.

In making decisions about what to do in this life we must take our blinders off and give serious consideration to the needs of others. Keeping my local neighbor in mind (e.g., charity begins at home) when choosing my options will help me develop a greater social awareness, but I must also work at broadening my vision to include all the peoples of the world. Our world has shrunk so much that no one can live even in national isolation. When deciding things that involve others, it must not be me first and you second. It's not what these countries and peoples can do for me. Rather, in Kennedy's famous words, it should be: What can I do for them?

*Points for Discussion and Reflection*

1. Do the people in your neighborhood (school, parish) have a good social awareness?

2. From the newspapers select stories that illustrate the social dimensions of human living.

3. Select instances from your own life and trace the impact these actions have had upon others.

4. What people had any great influence upon you and your values, attitudes, behavior? Why?

5. When management takes all the profits it can and when labor takes all the wages it can, what is left for company improvements? Has this had any effect upon American industry?

# Major Leaguers Forever

7

Little kids often dream about what they want to be when they grow up. Many do idolize athletes among others. But a good grade school athlete does not necessarily become a superstar. Stars are made, not born. It is true that some individuals have certain God-given talents that can never be taught them, especially reflex movements that great runners in football or great shooters in hockey seem to possess. The way to the big leagues, however, is long and arduous, and many fall by the wayside. There is one big difference, though, between becoming a major leaguer as an athlete and a mature person in real life. Major leaguers last only for a short number of years and then they have to retire. Mature, responsible people, it is hoped, will remain so forever.

## Maturation

Becoming adults in the full sense of the term does not occur just because we grow older. It is true that as the years go by we learn many things—manners, customs, values, prejudices, etc.—but only by hard work and patience do we turn this process into one of maturation. We grow in knowledge about what it is to live as a Christian in today's world. We have many experiences which challenge us to put our knowing into practice. We gradually achieve control over ourselves so that we can truly respond, and not react, to situations that develop. This proper maturing of the human person is what education and formation are all about. Education helps to form us by furnishing insights, by supplying reasons and motives for various ways of acting, by encouraging and rewarding proper human behavior. The

45

importance of personal and prayerful reflection can hardly be over-emphasized for anyone, and especially for a Christian. We arrive at the point where we have self-mastery so that when we see what is to be done, we do it without being told.

Dr. William C. Menninger lists the following criteria of emotional maturity. With a few minor additions to include our religious dimension, they would describe the behavior of mature Christians:

Having the ability to deal constructively with reality;

Having the capacity to adapt to change;

Having a relative freedom from symptoms that are produced by tensions and anxieties;

Having the capacity to find more satisfaction in giving than receiving;

Having the capacity to relate to other people in a consistent manner with mutual satisfaction and helpfulness;

Having the capacity to sublimate, to direct one's hostile energy into creative and constructive outlets;

Having the capacity to love.

The Prayer of St. Francis of Assisi says the same thing, but in a different way: "Lord, make me an instrument of thy peace; where there is hatred, let me sow love; where there is injury, pardon; where there is doubt, faith; where there is despair, hope; where there is darkness, light; and where there is sadness, joy. O divine Master, grant that I may not so much seek to be consoled as to console; to be understood as to understand; to be loved as to love with all my soul. For it is in giving that we receive, it is in pardoning that we are pardoned, and it is in dying that we are born to eternal life."

## Freedom

The characteristic that accurately describes a mature adult is freedom. In fact, we could call freedom the basic ingredient of all human morality and responsibility. We could never be held accountable—praised or blamed—for anything if we did not have a choice, if we were not free to do or not to do this.

Being free means that I have the capability of selecting my own goals in life and moving toward them. Since we are always in the pursuit of good, of that which satisfies our needs, freedom is essentially the power to do good. It is not really concerned with evil, except in that it has the power to overcome evil. We are most free when we easily and readily do what is right. It is a misuse to use it to accomplish evil, i.e., to sin.

Freedom is a positive thing. Even when we look upon freedom from fear, from poverty, from aggression, it is always with the understanding that only then will I be free for developing myself, my life, my family, my business. I will be free to do my own thing. I will be able to respond creatively with all my talents to the calls that come to me. Properly understood, each response of freedom should always be fresh, always new, always creative. I am constantly growing as a person and must respond with the new "me" to the challenge of this situation. That is why real people do not just do the same thing over and over again. For instance, saying "I love you" to one's spouse day after day never becomes boring or merely repetitive to a real person. It is always a new gift because I have grown and today can offer you still more than yesterday.

Freedom, though, is not an absolute thing. We are born free, i.e., we are born with the germ of freedom within us. The germ, though, has to be nurtured and it is going to be fostered within the built-in determinants not only of human nature, but specifically of this human person. Freedom will involve the acceptance of myself for what I am with all my limitations and of the providential circumstances in life, and the response to God's call to be "me" in the midst of this. It does not take a lot of thought for me to see that I have all kinds of limitations. I would still be in the first grade if I had to have an "A" in art and in music in order to move along to the second grade, and as I always tell my classes, half of us can never be mothers—or fathers!

What is so evident in regard to our physical selves is even more true with regard to our other faculties—emotions, intellect, will. Lack of education, improper formation, deficient motivation, undisciplined desires all hinder my acting freely. How can I freely make a good decision when I am missing half the facts? I need to be able to act in obedience to reason and not to my passions and desires. Temporary insanity, loss of temper, undisciplined desires for alcohol all have their negative impact upon my acting freely and maturely. I am free in the fullest sense if all my powers have reached their highest development and are able to act in their richest intensity.

In other words, there are obstacles to freedom. In addition to my own basic heritage—what I am born with and grow up with—there are a number of impediments to my acting freely and voluntarily in certain situations. Among these obstacles we can list ignorance, fear, violence, undisciplined passions, our past experiences. We cannot make free choices if we do not know what our options are or if we are not aware of the true nature of each option. We often think it might be neat to date a certain person, and then, we find out that he or she is really a bore. Fear—peer pressure, parental pressure, societal pressures of all kinds, fear of failing or not being accepted, etc.—can have its effects upon our decision making. Violence or force—rape, torture, threats to ourselves or to our families—makes us less free in our responses. Undisciplined passions or desires—addictions in varying degrees to alcohol, drugs, sex, food, sleep, etc.—hinder us from making completely free choices.

And there is always our past—both conscious and unconscious. So much of what we are and do as adults had its beginnings in our early years. Our first experiences as children, sudden shocking events, child abuse, rejection made their mark upon us. Repeated behavior developed certain patterns within us so that we do some things today quite automatically. We learned more than language as we grew up—attitudes, values, motives, virtues, how to survive. All these variables can affect our freedom today.

We must, however, keep in mind that although we are products of the past, we are not its prisoners. Our freedom gives us the capacity to recognize our weaknesses and to work at our personal growth and development. We overcome or counteract these various obstacles so that we can make personal choices for which we are held responsible.

## Responsibility

We use this term "responsibility" frequently as we refer to people acting responsibly or irresponsibly. Broken windows, unpaid bills, missing assignments, child abuse, driving while intoxicated, the nuclear arms race, are often called irresponsible. On the other hand, meeting one's car payments, class attendance, proper care of children, looking before crossing the street, not being involved in more activities than I can handle, are all cited as examples of responsible behavior.

In these instances and in others, irresponsible behavior will usually involve either not responding at all or not responding properly according to the total situation at hand. Responsible behavior will include accepting one's state of life, one's dignity, one's obligations and responding in a creative way to the demands of the moment. The whole process of maturation helps us to grow in self-determination and finally attain complete responsibility for our lives. We are accountable for all that we do. This does not mean that we never make mistakes. We do; but afterward we accept the responsibility. I was at fault in this traffic mishap and I shall pay for your car's repairs. We acknowledge our mistakes and take the proper steps to see to it that the mistakes are not repeated. We are perfectible creatures, not perfect ones.

In other words, we have arrived at the point where we respond rather than react to the challenges that we meet in our daily lives. This little comparison table succinctly points out what a response is—my creative answer to the demands of the present moment. I do not follow the leader, nor do I react instinctively as an animal might. I take charge; I make my own response which is truly an expression of myself.

The following four items are the basic ingredients in all responses: knowledge, values or convictions, self-discipline, crea-

| RESPONSE | REACTION |
|---|---|
| 1. thought out | 1. automatic, without thought |
| 2. creative | 2. instinctive |
| 3. accountable | 3. not always accountable |
| 4. distinctive of me; expresses me | 4. common to humans; expresses nature; or that part of nature that is in control right now |

tivity. I must know the situation in depth as well as in breadth. Just what is involved? What people are a part of it or will be affected by it? What effect can skipping classes have on my mastering of the course material? What are all the inner connections? The foreseeable consequences? A young couple may say they are mature enough to handle a sexual relationship. She becomes pregnant and they decide to have an abortion, because the baby would "interfere with their life-style." Responsible or not?

Much will depend on one's basic convictions or value system. Who am I? What are my basic values? What is truly important in my life? What are my obligations toward others: God, society, family, friends? Without basic values and convictions, there is no point of reference against which I can make good judgments. Not only must these convictions exist, but I must make them a part of me. I must see them for what they are. I must accept them as mine and not my parents' or church's. I must make them a part of me so that I am committed to living them.

Further, I need self-discipline, i.e., control of myself and my various faculties. Because of this I do not automatically jump to conclusions or instinctively reach out for something. I stop to look, to listen, to reflect. I realize there is more to the picture than what the eye may see or the ear may hear.

Finally, I can respond. I have a good grasp of all the facts involved. I see the various consequences—what impact the various options will have on my life and on the lives of others. I see how the options relate to my basic value system. I see how with my temperament, my personality, my talents, my very being, I can respond creatively so that this action truly expresses "me."

I act or I do not act. I am accountable for whichever I chose. I am responsible for the totality of the act—the means used, the basic effects, the natural consequences, the foreseeable effects. Being mature and placing one's neck on the line—I did it—is not always an easy thing to do, but it has its rewards, not the least of which is the sense of personal accomplishment. To live as a human being we need to accept ourselves and be proud of who we are and of what we do.

## Conscience

We are all familiar with the description of conscience as that little voice within us that (1) tells us to do or not to do something, and then (2) evaluates our behavior as good or bad. This voice should not be looked upon as something apart from us, nor should it be viewed merely as a part of us. This description is just that—a description to tell us what conscience does (prescribes and evaluates). In reality conscience is the personification of "me"; it is the expression of the stance that I take toward the challenges facing me with all their built-in obligations. It reflects accurately who I am and what I stand for.

It must always be listened to and followed. It is my innermost self directing me as to what I should do in order to attain my goals in life. It goes without saying, therefore, that the formation of a good conscience is part and parcel of the whole process of maturation discussed above. As mature persons we are expected to know who we really are and what we as Christians are supposed to accomplish with our lives. If we do not yet have this, we need the direction and counsel of more qualified people, e.g., parents and teachers. A properly formed conscience requires the following: a good value system, an attitude of reverence for life, awareness of the love triangle (i.e., the personal call of God to me and the demands of the community to which I belong), the ability to perceive, to evaluate, to decide and to prescribe. In other words, only a properly integrated person has it. This creation of the moral self or a truly virtuous person is the work of a lifetime. Having all our faculties developed, finely tuned and integrated into a balanced person is an ideal toward which we are constantly striving. That is why even adults with a formed conscience recognize the need at times to seek counsel on certain problems. Only at death do we stop being pilgrims, being perfectible.

## Decision-Making

Decision-making is the central act in all human morality. It is here where we gather ourselves together and make a commitment. We consider the situation; we gather knowledge; we sift through and evaluate the various options with their pros and cons. We then make our decision and commit ourselves to a way of acting.

It goes without saying that all of us need practice under capable guidance if we are ever to be turned loose on our own. As we grow we need to discuss problems and challenges in human living with people more experienced than ourselves. It is like being an apprentice in a kitchen, asking the master chef why this and why that, or like a rookie quarterback asking the veteran why he responded in the way that he did. We get to see what is involved in making enlightened decisions. We come to appreciate the tremendous power that is ours in being able to set in motion all the powers of a human being while committing oneself to performing a certain action or series of actions. We need practice, but not merely practice. A former music teacher of mine used to say, "Perfect practice makes perfect." That is why as we grow we work under the guidance of qualified persons who are capable of correcting our mistakes and who make good suggestions. A self-made individual can very easily be the product of unskilled labor—and show it.

## Passions

A part of us that does not always receive much attention these days is our passionate nature. It is basic to us and is that part of us that helps to make human living the joy it can be. We are not pure spirits. We have a rational appetite that enables us to seek after the spiritual or non-material goods of this life. As incarnate beings (integrated bodies and souls) we also have a sense appetite that seeks after the good of this life which can be perceived by our body nature. Technically, we call them passions or emotions, i.e., movements of the sense appetite, originating from the knowledge of good and evil, accompanied by some physical change. These movements begin in the soul, the seat of all human knowing, and terminate in the body. The knowledge does come via our senses. We "see" things that attract our attention, appeal to us as good and satisfying, and create a desire in us to possess them. Things that would come to us as unappealing we would seek to avoid. The physical changes that take place within us would be such things as increased heartbeat, goose pimples, red face, perspiration, etc.

Many of us blush when embarrassed, especially "us" blonds with such delicate sensitivities. Some individuals have a difficult time getting in front of people to talk. I went to school with someone who got diarrhea around exam time. Our heart beats faster when the object of our affections makes an appearance. Car enthusiasts light up when a Dusenberg rolls by.

It is natural for us to react to such stimuli. We like what is good; we dislike what is harmful. We can't wait for a free day; we postpone going to the dentist. We enjoy the company of a friend; we are bored to death by certain people—even teachers. However, if we just react (and not respond) we allow our body nature to take over and the passion can get out of hand. The out-of-control physical element can prove harmful. It can be a threat to our physical well-being. It will prevent concentration and will color all our impressions and judgments. It can also affect us so that we can't control ourselves, and our actions will prove to be un-Christian, e.g., violence when angry, cheating out of fear, etc.

Control of these passions is the mark of a mature person. We learn to take charge so that our reactions become responses. We learn to avoid situations that would upset us, to move out of the room before exploding in anger, to look upon things positively (when people talk about me they either say good things or lies!) and to control our bodies (count to ten, whistle while passing a place you fear, etc.). What we want to do is to control and direct our passions or emotions; we do not want to suppress them. Even our Lord got angry in the temple, but he controlled his reaction and turned it into a response. He did not treat each of the temple violators in the same way.

These passions that we are talking about describe the relationships we have to the presence of good and evil in our lives. In general we love what is good, desire it when it is absent, rejoice when it is present. If the good is something difficult to attain, hope buoys us up to move toward it while despair has us give up. In regard to evils that are difficult to avoid, courage helps us face up to them while fear makes us shrink away. When the difficult good is present, we rejoice all the more. When the difficult-to-avoid evil is present, we are more than sad—we are angry.

|  | Good |  | Evil |
| --- | --- | --- | --- |
| easy to attain/ avoid | love | general | hate |
|  | desire | absent | aversion |
|  | joy | present | sorrow |
| difficult to attain/ avoid | hope | | courage |
|  | | absent | |
|  | despair | | fear |
|  | | present | anger |

Growing up and integrating our life is a long and challenging task but it can be enjoyed. The more we appreciate who we are and what we can become, the more we appreciate the growing. In a way it is like a courtship. The pursuit of a great relationship can be most challenging but the end result makes it all worthwhile.

## Points for Discussion and Reflection

1. Why must a personal response be creative?
2. Is it more difficult today for young people to develop an authentic adult commitment?
3. What are some of the practical implications of the teaching on responsibility for parents, teachers, roommates? Am I my brother's/sister's keeper?
4. Discuss: Addiction to pills, alcohol, drugs is very destructive to human freedom.
5. Saints must be passionate people.
6. Give examples of the obstacles to freedom taken from the daily newspapers, TV programs, or your own life.
7. How do we know we have a conscience that is true and certain?
8. Discuss examples of "emotions at work" from your own life, from your own life, from TV programs, from the daily newspaper.

# Man-to-Man, Zone, Box and One

# 8

There is more than one kind of defense that a basketball coach can use in preparing a team for a game with one of his opponents. The heading of this chapter lists three of these, and there are many more. The coach considers his own players and their various competencies; he takes a long hard look at the opponents; he matches his players up against their opponents and makes a decision. In order to win this game the best defense for us to play is . . .

It is somewhat the same when it comes to moral decision-making. We all possess a basic philosophy of life which includes a set of values and convictions, a basic way of acting and making decisions. There are varieties of approaches to develop one's moral decision-making, but they will all use the same ingredients. Each approach must respect the person involved or it is not a good approach. However, each person is different; what is good for one may not be good for another; each person is called to be a unique original, not a carbon copy of someone else. The guiding principles and basic goodness or badness of specific actions must be kept in mind. Principles, though, are always incarnated in specific circumstances. These too must be respected for what they contribute to the overall understanding of the action here and now to be performed. Here we would like to share a few thoughts about three possible approaches: (a) law and order, (b) situational or contextual, (c) ideal.

## Law and Order

The law and order approach for the most part does not receive a good press today but it does have its positive points and

56

may be the best for certain people to follow. Children, for instance, usually follow this model until they are old enough to make their own decisions. This is also known as the authoritarian model, where authority figures make the decisions, give the orders, and we carry them out. There are a few advantages to this approach. First, authority usually has both the time and the competence to see the situation and all its implications—making what would be good decisions for the group or individual. Some of us either do not have the competence, or the time. It could also be that we do not want to take the time to think things out for ourselves. Parents usually make the decisions for their children; wives do the shopping for their husbands. And then, have you ever had trouble ordering in an unfamiliar restaurant? Or, how long does it take you to make your choice in an ice cream store with thirty-three different flavors?

Thus, in following this model, I can be assured of ready-made decisions. I save time and energy in not having to go through the decision-making process. I may find it difficult to live out the decisions made for me, but that is a small price to pay for all the help I have received.

This approach, however, does have its dangers: legalism, moralism and minimalism. These have to be recognized so that they can be avoided. In following the law, I do have to recognize that there can be exceptions. I can remember a Sunday morning back in the 1950's when I was serving the needs of the patients at a small hospital in the midwest; almost all were maternity cases. One woman wanted to go to confession. Why? I missed Mass this morning. Why? I was bringing my child into this world. Her strict legalistic upbringing made it difficult to reconcile any missing of Mass on a Sunday. It was always confessed, no matter what the reason.

Some authoritarians tend to moralize. My way of acting is the only correct way. If you do not do it as I direct you, you are sinning; you are going to be damned. Who are we to tell God what to do? How positive can I be that this law and order approach in all its literalness is the only Christian way to live? God sees the heart; God knows whether we are loving him. I am not able to say that in all instances you are wrong and God will send you to hell. Laws should never be canonized and I should never place myself above God. This does not mean I can do as I please. It just recognizes that at times there may be more than one way to live out the dictates of the law.

Then there are the minimalists. These people accept the law but then study it so as to see what least response they have to make in order to meet the basic demands of the law. What do I have to do before I sin? Law only imposes the minimum upon me; what is it? When I become a strict legalist I commit myself to observe the law. However, the generous side of me is not appealed to, only the necessary side. I want to observe the law, but am not inclined to do more than I have to. Minimalists follow the letter of the law; they do what they have to in order to get by. They will condemn "big sins" (what we used to call mortal sins) but they can easily get into the habit of accepting little sins as an ordinary part of their lives.

## Situational/Contextual

One thing that we have learned over the years is that we are all different. What fits you does not necessarily fit me. In making decisions, we need to keep in mind our entire person, all facets of our being. We are not pure spirits. We have as many sides as Rubik's cube and and putting them all together is not easy. We need to take care of our physical needs (health, food, sleep), our intellectual stimulation (education, good reading, some TV), our emotional well-being (proper love, care, respect), our social relationships (loneliness can be a terrible thing), our cultural background (and not just art and music in our leisure hours), and our moral behavior (which is involved in all the preceding).

Erma Bombeck some years ago wrote a beautiful column on "the child I love the most." At first the reader may be surprised, but then who else can it be? The child I love the most is always the one in need—the five year old running a high fever, the nine year old who struck out four times in a little league game, the seventeen year old dateless on prom night.

58

Before we make decisions we must know the facts. Circumstances do change the picture and our decisions will not always be the same. Things are not all black and white; they do differ from person to person. My trifocals will not do your eyes much good. We are not all on the same diet. In order to make proper decisions that respect the individuality of both the person and the situation, many people prefer to follow a "contextual or situational" approach to morality.

At first glance this does seem to fit the bill. It makes us take into consideration the concrete circumstances when we make a decision. But what should we do about the basic law or principle involved? Some extremists here would say: Forget about it. If the principle does not seem to help you make a decision, toss it aside and look for something else. When all else fails, just do the loving thing (whatever that is). This extremist situation ethic could be seen as just "do your own thing." Whatever you decide to do is O.K. Do it! I often wonder what these people do when taking tests. Put down whatever you think and you will be right? That never worked with me—neither when I was a student nor now that I am a teacher.

However, when we put the two (rule and circumstances) together into a dialectical relationship we come up with something else. I first came upon this discovery when I was preparing a homily for a wedding. I knew that Jane would have some appropriate comments to make if she found out that I had dusted off a used homily. So I kept reflecting on different texts, and especially the Marcan text on how the two become one. How is this possible? 1 + 1 = 2? No. After some more prayerful reflection it came to me: $1 \times 1 = 1$! This sums up what marriage is all about. There have to be two wholes; both have to give their all. There are no half-way commitments; no partial giving is sufficient. The two spouses are in dynamic relationship ("$\times$"). The plus sign ($+$) indicates addition but no interaction. A pile of rocks, a shelf of books, a bushel of peaches, fifty students packed into a car are all the result of one being added to another. Being stacked one on top of another does not say much about personal union. You are physically in contact with people on a crowded subway but you are not personally pres-

59

ent to them, united to them and interacting with them. This dialectic is most important; it is this interaction which produces union. Neither spouse is swallowed up by the other; there is no disregard of the other. The integrity of both is respected and maintained. Otherwise there is no real marriage. A husband and wife, two separate unique individuals, strive to create a special union without destroying their own persons. At times I think the union of the divine and human natures in Jesus Christ is a helpful illustration of this.

The same is true in human behavior. We have principles and we have concrete situations. The two need to be brought together. What better description than a marriage of principles and circumstances $(1 \times 1 = 1)$. We are never allowed to discard the principle nor are we allowed to ignore the demands of the concrete situation. We need to keep the totality of both, if not in the letter, certainly in spirit. This relationship is not a case of 50-50 but of 100-100, even though at times principles seem to be on top (130-70), and at other times the circumstances are. The principles and circumstances interact upon each other, and when viewed properly they produce a clear total picture.

See what answer this concept of $1 \times 1$ gives us in regard to the woman giving birth to her child on Sunday. Yes, we should worship the Lord with our faith community, and this means gathering together on Sunday to celebrate Mass. This is a serious obligation for all who understand their relationship with God and the community. However, it is not an absolute; there are exceptions. Our $1 \times 1$ does not say it is O.K. to skip Mass any time I feel like it. No, I hold to community obligations, but I realize that in this instance the value of giving proper attention to the birth of my baby takes precedence over celebrating Mass with my community. The integrity of both the principles and the situations are maintained 100% but I do not give birth to my baby in a church!

In making decisions of a moral nature, no matter what they are, we must give serious consideration to the basic principles involved (law, rules, tradition) and to the concrete circumstances. In a way, we have always done this even if we did not always look upon it as "$1 \times 1$." We knew there was a difference between stealing $5 and $5,000; between sleeping with my wife and my neighbor's; between missing Mass because of sickness and out of laziness. This contextual approach of $1 \times 1 = 1$ respects all the ingredients while challenging us to become the best that we can be.

## The Ideal

A third approach to moral decision-making centers on the ideal. Properly understood, this challenges a Christian to the utmost. Improperly understood, it can be seen as a pious platitude that speaks big and does little. It makes us appear as though we are committed to being the best possible Christian but since it is not realizable we settle down into a minimal morality at best—after all, we tried! It is perhaps for this reason that this approach is not an acceptable model for certain Christians. But let's look at the ideal from a positive point of view and see what it has to offer us.

The ideal is the expression of the most perfect human behavior possible. It sets forth the behavior that may possibly be attained only under perfect conditions. Since we live in a finite world where such conditions do not exist, it is not realizable. If it were, it would not be an ideal for long. Once we reached it we would have to set another. Our ideal is truly an impossible one. What did Christ tell us? Be perfect as your Father in heaven is perfect. Do any of us really think that we can be as good, as loving, as perfect as God? No way—but it does give us something to strive toward. The important point is not getting *there* but *getting* there. We are pilgrims on the road toward our goal of perfection. We are doing the best that we can—some crawling, some walking, some running, and maybe some flying along. We are headed in the right direction. The fact that we stumble and fall is not so important, unless we are deliberately tripping others or ourselves. We do not worry if some are running faster. What does count is whether I am running as well as I can right now. The following chart summarizes the big differences between ideal (maximal) morality and minimal morality:

| IDEAL | | MINIMAL |
|---|---|---|
| best possible me | GOAL | get by |
| all I have; never stops | EFFORT | just what is necessary; soon stops |
| a guide; spirit | LAW | letter |
| understands but does not approve; encourages us to grow | SIN | condemns if "mortal," tolerates all others |

The ideal morality insists that we become the best possible person we can become. We cannot stop working toward this goal until we die. As long as we are alive we can give a little more. Laws are looked upon as a guide, pointing us in the right direction. We try to live their spirit as fully as we can. When it comes to sin, the ideal morality does not condemn us (unless we are hypocrites). It understands whatever mistakes we made, but it does not say: good, O.K., go and do it again. Instead it lets us know that this is not the way to act, but we know that you are human and you do make mistakes. As long as this is the best you can do right now, O.K.; but get back up and work a little harder. You *can* do better.

That is why in presenting any teaching on moral matters we get further by presenting the ideal. This is what we are striving toward; this is what ideal human Christian behavior would be. For instance, marriage is indissoluble; natural family planning is the ideal method; wealth should be distributed equitably; there should be equal opportunities for all. What is demanded is that each of us strive to reach that ideal. We do all we can to help ourselves get there and facilitate others in their quest. We must do all we can to set up the societal and cultural conditions that will enable, encourage, support, and stimulate such endeavors.

This is a far cry from a legalistic approach which settles down to the minimal.

This is why we say we make the best possible decision we can make now. We look at the problem from all sides. We take into consideration all our own capabilities. We realize that we are not perfect and that we may need to change tomorrow. We decide according to the total picture available to us. We must make our decisions now; we cannot put them off; we make the best one possible. At the same time we remain open. We are perfectible; we are pilgrims; we are sinners; we do make mistakes. After acting we do reflect upon what we have done and often see things in a clearer light. We know what to do next time. When possible, we consult others more qualified than ourselves. If new prophets come along to give us better insights into the total situation, we listen to them and make the necessary adjustments.

We still will focus on making the best possible decision we can make now, in the light of all the information available to us and with a view of coming just a little bit closer to our ideal. Our satisfaction is not in realizing the unattainable ideal, but in fully activating all our talents and potentialities.

The above are only three of the many models available, and even these three can exist in various combinations. A person may even use all three but under different circumstances. Whichever model or models we choose to make our own, we should keep in mind that it should help us to become a unique original. It should stimulate us toward our ideal and it must respect the integrity of the person, of the law and of the circumstances.

### Points for Discussion and Reflection

1. Discuss: This is a hard saying, and who can hear it?
2. Discuss: We grow to adulthood very gradually.
3. Apply the ideal response vs. the minimal response to concrete situations in your life.
4. Which approach discussed is the most "Christian"? Why?

5. Which is the best approach for me? Why?
6. What must a good standard of morality take into consideration? Why?
7. The way-out new morality can reflect much infantilism.
8. Is conscience the lawmaker or the interpreter of laws?

# Game Plans

## 9

Coaches of athletic teams always want their players to play up to their abilities and thus probably to win the game. They want to capitalize on their own team's strong points as well as to exploit the other team's weaknesses. In preparing their teams for a game they devise strategies or game plans. If their teams are able to execute the game plan as designed, there is always an excellent chance for them to win the game. The game of life is no different. We all need to put together the proper elements into a well-designed game plan, which can vary from person to person, and then go out and execute it.

## Healthy (Virtuous) Human Beings

The whole process of human maturation has as its goal the development of a healthy human being—one who possesses as good a physical health as possible, one who is mentally stable, one who is virtuous. A virtuous person is one who has power, i.e., one who has harnessed his/her various faculties under the proper guidance of a clear and unbiased vision. Such an individual sees clearly and is able to carry out the directions given. Another way of saying this is that such a person is the possessor of a good value system, a good decision-making apparatus, and has himself/herself under control so that he/she can act Christianly and not just biologically or humanly.

## Values

Value is tied in with worth or deserving to be wanted. A diamond ring is valuable because it is worth $5,000. A college education is valuable because it opens the door to many well paying jobs. This rosary, now falling apart, is valuable to me because it was my mother's. My portrait hanging in my office is somewhat of a conversation piece. Why is that priest wearing a UD beanie? To a close friend of mine, the portrait is priceless! She wants me to leave it to her in my will. A fifty cent key may open the doors to some very valuable works of art. In brief, some things have value in themselves and deserve to be wanted. Other items may not have intrinsic value, but either because of their connection with someone or because they are a means to something else, they can be strongly wanted by certain people.

All of us have values. We all want something. We all place the attainment or retention of some things above others. What we value says something about us. A small child prefers a large nickle to a little dime, a shiny red toy to a dull green one. Physical charm is more appealing to some people than is deep inner beauty. Honesty and integrity are more important than economic or academic success. Our values may not always be the best and we may not always have a good sense of their relative importance, but they are there. We have picked them up at home, at school, at church, at play, from the media, from friends, etc.

Part of the process in growing up is to sort all of this out. We gradually get a better grasp of what it is to be me, as this unique person, related to God and neighbor. We pick up more and more the basics of our human condition. We realize more accurately what is important in life and the worth of the various teachers we have encountered. We soon find out that we become like those with whom we associate, and if we are to call ourselves Christians, we have to take upon ourselves Christian values and patterns of behavior.

As followers of Christ we must get to know him as well as we can. Scripture is to be read and reflected upon regularly. We must make Jesus a part of our lives so that we think more like him, take on his attitudes, and approach life situations as he would.

Christians for twenty centuries have been endeavoring to live the Christ life. Their lives bear witness to what is important. The teachings of great people (bishops, etc.) show how the faith is to be lived in the context of the circumstances of the times.

The Church community today gives us new formulations of the basic traditional values. Listening to all of them helps us distill out the basic values and gives us insights into how they are to be lived today.

As adults we are to have a sense of values, i.e., we have values and we have to prioritize them. This does not mean establishing a static order of what always comes first, second, etc. Values are in dynamic relationship with one another and with me. They are constantly striving for my attention. (Recall Erma Bombeck's "The Child I Love the Most.") Thus, today, Tuesday, I get up and go to school; Saturday I sleep in. We do not neglect any of the values; at times it is necessary to give top priority to this one because of these overriding reasons. No value can be ignored and forgotten about; otherwise it would cease to be a value.

The Christian community has its fundamental values based on what it means to be a follower of Christ. We are God's; we are gifted both in ourselves and in what we possess. We are given stewardship over valuable gifts, and after using them for the greater honor and glory of God and his creatures, we are to return them to God. They are never ours!

Human life is one of these values. Existence is a gift of God. I am created as a unique individual with my own talents and personality. No one else is like me. I am a steward but not an absolute owner. I cannot dispose of myself as I will, but according to the overreaching plans of God. I am called to grow and make my contributions to society, to all of God's kingdom. I am called to respond to God and therefore have the capability of making my own decisions. I must take care of my life (health, drinking, drugs, etc.). I must respect the lives of others, including the unborn (no killing, assault, harm), and all of God's creation (plants, animals, minerals, etc.), using them only in ways that enhance life.

Human dignity is another value. I am someone special and so are you. Just think about what this implies for the way we should treat each other, the way we should talk to and about each other, the language we should use, the non-pollution of the environment, our social relationships from friendly associations to snubbing one another, business and labor relations, working conditions, exploitation of third world peoples, discrimination on basis of sex, race, creed, or whatever. And Christ said: "Whatever you do to them, you do to me."

A third value is human sexuality. It is a basic part of my total being, and over which I have stewardship. I must use it in the proper context. As social beings, we use our bodily powers (eyes, voice, hands, etc.) to express ourselves to others and vice versa. Sexual acts have a proper meaning and are to be used as expressions of real love. Misuse destroys the meaning that is built into them.

## Biologically, Humanly, Christianly

In actualizing our various faculties and using the various gifts over which we are stewards we are able to act in various ways. For the sake of our discussion, let's call three of them biological, human and Christian ways of acting. Just what is the difference?

We are body-soul persons. We eat, drink, sleep, rest, procreate. We take care of all our bodily needs and functions, but we do not act only as "bodies" or biologically. If we did, we would act as animals, out of instinct and in accord only with that body part of us. Our health habits are also determined by what we are as persons and by our total needs of the moment. We may be tired but we study for a test instead of going to bed early. We may be hungry but we cut down on how much we eat because we need to lose weight, or even a penance for some past mistakes (ours or others). St. Francis Xavier, we are told, used to give his penitents very minor penances but would then inflict great ones upon himself as a reparation for their sins. The mating urge in animals is governed by instinct. Human beings can have intercourse at times other than when the woman would get pregnant. Thus, we can have all kinds of physical urges, but we do not react to them; we respond. This is the big difference between acting biologically (only taking into account our physical nature) and humanly (considering the total person from a human standpoint).

When we act as a human being, we consider the whole person, including our relationships with others. We can even go without because of the needs of others. Many a mother goes without so that her child can have a new pair of shoes. We decide what action to take after we consider the needs and values of the entire person. What would be good for the total me in this situation? We may have to sacrifice satisfying a physical urge because of higher ranking needs and values. The self-discipline engaged in by athletes in training is a good example. Married people with a sick spouse very easily control their sexual desires; they do not insist on sexual relations with a substitute because their spouse is sick or out of town.

When we add the faith dimension of a Christian (being specially gifted by God with a share in the divine life and with a call to live a life of total love) we may further change some of our behavior patterns. Christ himself told us that the world would consider us foolish rather than wise in what we do. The secular world does not appreciate the celibacy of priests, the vows lived by religious, the dedication of many people serving the poor and the sick for "nothing." Making decisions because we are faith-filled Christians, i.e., sons and daughters of God, will lead to far different choices. I can remember being called foolish because I turned down a college scholarship in order to enter religious life. Take the scholarship, get your education; protect yourself in case you decide not to be a religious. The work of Mother Teresa and her cohorts, serving poor, unwanted, dying people, is not easily understood by those with a "this world" mentality. In the same way, decisions to worship the Lord with my faith community on a Sunday morning, to be a good steward of the goods of this world by not getting drunk, to revere my sexuality and yours by not satisfying my natural urges, are not easily appreciated by the worldly minded. We act biologically, humanly or Christianly insofar as we have a value system and consequent activity that is based on us as physical bodies, as human beings, or as persons specially gifted by God in our nature and in our calling. The chart on p. 70 summarizes these three different activities.

In sum, Christian values for the most part are basic human values seen in the light of the fact that we come from God and

|  | BIOLOGICALLY | HUMANLY | CHRISTIANLY |
|---|---|---|---|
| Directed by: | Instinct | Reason | Faith, Holy Spirit |
| Acting as: | "Animal" Physical needs | Whole person, including social needs | Child of God; religious dimension |
| Actions are: | Reactions | Responses | Movements of the Spirit |

are destined to return to him. We see all things as gifts from God, over which we are stewards, and which are to be used for the honor and glory of God and the good of our neighbor, i.e., to be used properly as a means of helping us and our brothers and sisters attain our goal in life—God. In our operation and use of all valuable things (everything has value) we recognize the difference between acting biologically, humanly and Christianly.

### Recipe for Virtue

As a conclusion to this chapter I would like to offer a recipe for the inculcation of good moral habits. Most of us recognize the fact that we are not perfect and that we do need to develop our good side. We have our faults and we can spend a lot of time just pulling weeds. I think it is much more rewarding to plant flowers. Thus, once we have identified our problem and what we want to do, i.e., what good moral habit we want to develop, we can follow this recipe in seven steps. When reading through the following it is recommended that you select a particular problem of your own and make specific applications of each step. At the end a concrete example will be given in order to show how the recipe could work.

1. *Build up Grace.*
We need to be healthy if we are to be strong enough to avoid

mistakes and to do good things. We get sick much more readily when we are physically run down. In the same way, we have to build up our relationship with God, our sharing in the life he offers us. How can we do this? There are various ways, but here are a few suggestions.

a. *Prayer*: Prayer is the expression of our love life with God. Lovers flourish when they share their love. We need to express this relationship frequently throughout the day—the sharing of what we are doing, our feelings, our ups and downs.

b. *Sacraments*: In the Catholic tradition, these are special means of contact with God. Regular use of the sacrament of reconciliation keeps us aware both of our own human imperfections and of the help that God offers us. Frequent reception of the Eucharist helps our life with God to grow, just as hugs and kisses do.

c. *Devotion to Mary and the Saints:* These are special members of God's kingdom. Since we become like those with whom we associate, regular contact with these friends of ours and of God helps us develop the right attitudes. It is usually easy to chat with a mother or with friends.

2. *Create an Atmosphere of God's Presence.*

God is present everywhere. When we are aware that God is here, we act accordingly. We can help create this awareness by making acts of faith and love throughout the day; by the use of such things as a crucifix, a medal, a picture; by the use of reminders written on small slips of paper that can be inserted in books we use, in our desk, on our mirror, etc. Our contacts with God enable us to build up grace.

3. *Realize My Dignity.*

Actions flow from convictions. If we are convinced that we are children of God, that we are called to intimate love relationships with him, we start living up to it. We can spend a few minutes in prayer every morning and evening, reflecting on who we are as children of God. We can repeat many times a day: I am a daughter/son of God.

4. *Strengthen My Will.*

We are weak; we lack complete self-control. Our spiritual

muscles just aren't there sometimes. This is a result of our basic humanness (we are born weak) and of our bad habits, our failures to work at getting ourselves into shape. We need to start exercising every day with several acts of self-denial.

5. *Punish the Failure.*

Even though hugs are better than slugs, reparation for faults is necessary. This makes an impression upon us and we think twice before repeating the same mistake. When possible, we should fit the punishment to the crime. If we were uncharitable, do something kind for the person. If we overindulge, give up a few beers.

6. *Positive Good Actions.*

Plant flowers rather than pull weeds. If we have a garden plot and only pull weeds, all we have is mud. If we plant flowers, we have something nice to look at, there is less room for weeds, and we are more inclined to pull the weeds which interfere with the beauty of the flowers. If we are working at being more charitable in speech, make it a point every day to say something nice about somebody.

7. *Guidance.*

We are born weak, uninformed and underdeveloped. As we grow, we make good use of all kinds of help from qualified people. As we work on developing good moral habits, we can use a spiritual advisor. We need a friend, experienced in spiritual matters, who can help us. We need to be able to sit down and talk out our problems with someone who will accept us for who we are and help us become our full selves. At times, this could be our regular confessor (if we frequent the sacrament of reconciliation—step 1), and can take place at the same time or it can occur anywhere at any time—over a beer or a cup of coffee, in an office or out in the park. Remember, a self-made person is often a product of unskilled labor.

## Application of the Recipe to a Particular Problem

*Problem:* Uncharitable comments about others, especially Joe and Judy

*Goal:* Develop habit of only making charitable comments about others

1. Build up grace
   a. Morning and night prayers each day without fail
   b. One visit to school chapel every day
   c. Five minute reading of Bible each night before retiring
   d. Mass and Communion twice a week on Sundays and Wednesdays
   e. Confession every two months; Fr. Joe will be my confessor
   f. At morning and night prayers discuss my problem with the Lord and our Blessed Mother

2. Create an atmosphere of God's presence
   a. Wear my small cross; touch it ten times a day and say "I believe God is here with me."
   b. Write "God is here" on a slip of paper and insert it in my assignment book.

3. Realize my dignity
   a. Ten times each day I shall repeat: I am a son of God, Joe is a son of God, Judy is a daughter of God.

4. Strengthen my will
   a. Five times a day I shall sit up straight in my chair for 15–20 seconds.
   b. Once each day I shall give up something to drink, even if if only a drink of water.

5. Punish the failure
   a. Every time I say something uncharitable about Joe (or Judy or anyone) I shall make reparation by saying something positive about him.

6. Positive good actions
   a. Three times each day I shall say something kind to or about another person.

7. Guidance
   a. I shall talk over this problem with Fr. Joe and keep in touch with him monthly.

*Points for Discussion and Reflection*

1. Discuss: Growth in values is an unfinished symphony.

2. Are the born-again Christians on the right track in placing so much emphasis on accepting Christ as one's Lord and Savior? Why?

3. Select a problem in your own life (or in the life of a friend) and work out the seven steps recipe to show how they would apply in developing a precise good moral habit.

4. How does hero worship affect the formation of our habits? Who are some living personalities you would recommend as models?

5. List your own personal values. Where did you get them? Which ones are the most important to you? Why?

# A Summary

Kitchens have different arrangements, but they have the same basic equipment. Cookbooks abound, but the essentials remain the same. Drill teams basically perform the same maneuvers but add their own little twists. Football teams use the same basic formations and plays but execute them in a slighlty different manner. In the same way books on morality and ethics will take the same fundamental material and arrange it differently and give special emphasis to certain points. In this book I have developed at length what I have called elsewhere a contemporary Christian ethic in ten points (cf. *Catholicism Today*, pp. 133-136.) The points here, though, are totally rearranged.

## Contemporary Christian Ethic

The ten points that make up what I entitle an ethic for contemporary Christians are these:

1. God is our Creator. God, incarnate as Jesus, is the revelation of what it means to be a human being. God is our Redeemer; God is our fulfillment.
2. A Christian's morality is the way he/she acts in freely responding to God, who invites all of us to enter into a personal love relationship with him as members of his kingdom.
3. A Christian morality is a morality of love of God, of neighbor, and of self.
4. A Christian morality is a challenging morality. In being ourselves, we strive to become our full selves and unique originals.
5. A Christian is responsible for the full impact of his/her actions.

6. A mature Christian must be properly formed; we are not born mature. No one is absolutely free but we can work to develop our capacity for freedom and then exercise it.
7. A Christian operates within the context of a dynamic constellation of values, not a static pyramid. We make our decisions in the light of the entire person who can be summed up by these descriptive terms: individual, religious, incarnate, social historical, or perfectible.
8. A Christian looks to the following for the formation and understanding of his/her values: Christ, the Christian community of yesterday as well as that of today, the insights of other religions, cultures, the sciences, plus personal and prayerful reflection.
9. A Christian follows a morality of tension—a marriage of principles and circumstances.
10. A sincere Christian makes the best possible decision that can be made right now, and at the same time remains open to growth and change tomorrow.

## Six Essential Ideas

If I were to single out several points which I think are very essential to the approach to morality presented here I would list the following six items.

1. *Our God-relatedness:* God created us, giving us our specific nature, talents and calling. We are to exercise stewardship over all these gifts as we move toward our goal in life, attaining a deep personal love relationship with our God as members of his kingdom. God created this game of life and set down its basic nature and rules.

2. *Triangle of love:* Love is the key to the fullness of human existence and should be descriptive of all our behavior. However, it is triangular. All love must relate us at one and the same time and in a positive way to God, to our neighbors and to ourselves.

3. *Unique originals:* As human beings we all possess the same basic nature and calling. Yet we are unique individuals, called to live our own particular existence and fulfill our Chris-

tian calling within the dimensions of the specific gifts and talents we each have been given. Our living must truly be personal.

4. *1 × 1 = 1*: Life is complicated. Few laws admit of universal simple applications. Because of our own uniqueness we discover that our life is composed of a multitude of particular situations. In making our decisions we need to maintain the integrity of the Christian principles as well as respect the challenge of the concrete circumstances of life.

5. *Challenge of the ideal*: We are all called to be something special as we follow in the footsteps of Christ. Our calling is to be perfect as our Father in heaven is perfect. This ideal challenges us to become the best possible person we can be and to make full use of all our talents and gifts.

6. *Plant flowers*: It is much more enjoyable and profitable to plant flowers than to pull weeds. Emphasis in good Christian living should not be on the avoidance of sin, but rather on the performance of positive good actions. We love by loving, not by avoiding, though the fullness of love will include avoiding those things that harm the ones we love (God, neighbor, self).

These six points give a distinctiveness to the Christian morality as described in these pages. Properly incorporated into any Christian's way of life, they should enable everyone to become the best possible person he or she can be. Carried out to their perfection they should have a tremendous impact upon the moral climate not only of our own little ghetto but of the whole world.

## Traditional Approach

A comparison with the so-called traditional overview as presented by Thomas Aquinas (thirteenth century) and developed by others over the years will show that the differences are not in substance but in the manner of presentation. I like to summarize this traditional approach in six brief sentences. We are; we act; we become; we learn; we fall; we live. A look at what is included under each one of these points shows how much basic agreement exists as far as content is concerned.

1. *We are.* We exist as creatures of God and are destined

for happiness. All of us are capable of attaining happiness. We will find it only in God and not in any created good, though many of us will try to do so.

2. *We act.* We are responsible persons capable of acting deliberately on our own. Although we are free, there are impediments that can interfere—ignorance, fear, violence, concupiscence or passions. Our human actions are likewise moral. To see this fully we look at the basic nature of the action, its various circumstances (who, what, where, when, why, how, by what means) and especially the reason why we are doing it. We then see how all this fits in with the basic standards—God's eternal law, the dictates of human reason, our own conscience.

The passionate side of our nature must also be treated because it can have quite an effect upon our overall responsibility. We have emotions, passions or sense appetites which react to the presence of good and evil in our lives. These passions are treated in general and then in particular—love and hate, desire and aversion, joy and sadness, hope and despair, fear and courage, anger.

3. *We become.* At birth we have no habits. As we grow, we develop our various powers and form all kinds of habits—body habits, study habits, health habits, etc. Proper "human" habits, or virtues, are the internal principles of good living, a "second nature" which helps us to act readily and naturally for the good.

4. *We learn.* We are born, as they say, with a blank slate. We need to learn all about life and human relationships. We need laws and teachers, whether they be road maps, telephone books, cookbooks, logarithm tables, moral guidelines.

5. *We fall.* The mystery of iniquity or sin shows up in our lives in all kinds of shapes and forms.

6. *We live.* We are not only human, but are called to a special life of friendship with God. For this, we need to share in God's life in a unique way which we call grace.

All these points in the traditional approach are broken down logically into their various component parts (nature, definition, kinds or divisions, causes, effects, etc.) and each is treated in turn.

## Points for Discussion and Reflection

1. What analogy, either one of those used in this book or another of your own choice, would you use to present Christian morality? Why?

2. Do you like the traditional approach? Why?

3. Do you agree that the six points selected are the fundamental ones presented in this book?

4. Are we interpreting Jesus Christ in the way he should be interpreted?

5. Draw up your own code of ethics for a contemporary Christian.

# Appendix
# Particular Issues

Most treatises on morality are divided into two major parts—morality in general and morality in particular. The first part (morality in general) is pretty much what we have been talking about up until now—a presentation of those elements common to all moral issues. In treating morality in particular, authors would then examine specific moral topics, either by following the ten commandments and discussing the various moral problems related to each commandment in turn, or by taking the basic virtues (faith, hope, charity, prudence, justice, fortitude and temperance) and treating the various moral questions involved with each. A further breakdown today would lead to detailed treatment of specialized areas such as medical ethics, business ethics, engineering ethics, legal ethics, etc.

In this appendix we shall select only three areas that are a part of our lives (daily living or campus morality; Christian sexuality; peace and justice) and give presentations of each. These will be very short sketches meant to serve as an introduction to further discussion and fuller development. What is done here for these three topics can be done for many others.

# Illustration One:
# Daily Living

This first discussion deals with the moral behavior we are exposed to in our ordinary everyday living. The basic principles involved would apply to all peoples in all neighborhoods. In reading these few pages you can make the necessary application to your community. Here many of the examples will be drawn from campus living.

If we look around ourselves, what do we see? "See how they love one another" was said of the early Christians. Would the same apply to us? If an alien from another planet came to earth on a scouting mission, and especially of this neighborhood, what kind of report would "he" make about us? What kind of people are we?

What would our visitor look at, especially since he will make this report only by viewing what we do rather than by asking us what we think we are? As a start we could suggest that the alien consider the following questions: What is their environment like? How do they take care of it (neatness, pollution, litter, etc.)? How do they exercise dominion over the material things of this earth—furniture, buildings, property, food, alcohol? How do they use their time and measure up to their responsibilities? How do they treat each other? Are they respectful and considerate? What is their ordinary language like? How do they take care of themselves (body, soul, spirit)?

In doing so, our visitor would be given some insights into the way we view one another, the dignity we accord each other, the way we respect the rights of others, our stewardship over material things. Do we have true reverence and respect for all of God's creation? Do we use all for the greater honor and glory of our Creator? Do we acknowledge in our daily lives that there is someone above us? Are we absolute owners over all? How responsible are we toward all creation?

The alien goes around our neighborhood for a week or two and jots down some observations. If we peeked at his notes, what would we see? On the plus side we might find items leading to the conclusion that we are a Christian community. For example, we are a very friendly campus and everyone is made to feel at home. The students are very interested in helping others; many are members of at least one service club of which there are a dozen or so. Attendance and participation at worship services are not perfect but they are quite good; retreats are well attended. The alien might wonder though about how serious people are about their spiritual growth and how well they use the means afforded them.

On the negative side there would be more than a few question marks and exclamation points next to various items. What about the litter and debris? Are the student parties always the ones you would invite Jesus to? Would we be asking Christ for another Cana or would we be too far gone to even ask? Do our celebrations respect the rights of others, i.e., noise level in the wee hours of the morning? Do we respect the rights of fellow students to a bit of quiet time for study? Do we impose our smoking on the non-smokers? Do we pull fire alarms in the middle of the night? Do we respect the property of others, including the school—dorm damages, marked-up desks, signs painted on others' property? Do we waste things? What report would our visitor make after walking with the pledges all through pledge period, including hell week? If all our dorm conversations were tape-recorded, how would we rate on vocabulary and charitableness, just to mention two items?

Making out a final report would not be easy. Just how alert are the students, faculty and staff in what they do? Are they just going through the motions and following the crowd, or do they deliberately do these things, both the good and bad? Just how much pressure is there? How mature are the students? Are they capable of handling the challenges of being on their own? How responsible are they for their sisters and brothers? They call themselves Christians. How are they measuring up to what the visitor finds contained in the New Testament?

What would the final evaluation be?

## Points for Discussion and Reflection

1. Is my campus/school/neighborhood a Christian one? How would you go about answering this? What values are involved? What questions would you seek to answer? What conclusions did you come to? Why?

2. Has not the assumption that human beings are the highest order of creation contributed to our misuse of things around us?

3. What steps would you take in order to make your own neighborhood a little more Christian in nature?

4. Write a preliminary draft of the report the alien visitor would make of your own neighborhood or school community.

# Illustration Two:
# Christian Sexuality

The basic question underlying all sexuality may be expressed as follows: Is this sexual act truly an expression of the love we have for each other? The answer is very involved. Even before we deal with the question itself, we need to consider a number of background items: who we are as individuals, as followers of Christ, as members of a church community; friendship and its expressions.

First of all, who am I and who are you? What is our basic relationship to self, to others, to God? Why did God make us? What does it mean to be a person? What goes into the making of me? How many parts are there and which of them must I keep in mind? What does it mean to be a responsible self?

How grown up am I? Am I a virtuous person, i.e., someone with a broad vision and a highly developed self-discipline? A broad vision takes in all sides of the question in an unbiased way. To be disciplined, an individual has to integrate all one's faculties (body, soul, heart, emotions, etc.) into a well-balanced whole that responds readily and correctly to the commands of a Christian conscience. We all become pregnant with faith and adulthood. Have we given birth to the adult or are we still searching for what it is to be a full-fledged Christian, totally responsible in a Christian way for all we do?

We are Christians. We are to live today the Christ event experienced by the early Christians. Christ had a tremendous impact upon their lives and they changed their manner of living. Christ's teachings are to be lived by us today. Does he have anything to say about being human, about being responsible for making good use of all the gifts given to us? How does sex fit into the lives of good Christians?

Is the Church always right? Has Christian tradition always correctly understood sexuality? It is evident that the Church is dependent upon other sciences for knowledge of sex and its biological functions. In its approach to various questions, the Church is also influenced by various cultural phenomena. The Church throughout its history has been composed of human beings who do not have the whole truth. Only God does. Just because the Church's knowledge is incomplete, however, does not mean that all its teachings are wrong. Rather, it shares with its members the fullness of the truth insofar as it has grasped that truth at this stage of history. For instance, in past years we thought that sex was either for making babies or satisfying physical urges. Ruling out babies left lustful pleasure, and this did not seem to be proper for a good Christian. For centuries our Western (and Christian) approach to the physical world and its pleasures was negative, to say the least. Only in recent times have we developed a greater appreciation for all that the physical world has to offer. Our knowledge of sexuality has grown so that we can see that it encompasses not only babies and physical pleasure, but, just as importantly, self-communication and intimacy between lovers.

Friends grow in their relationship as they communicate more deeply with their partners. They can do this in various ways. Some use words; others, looks; still others, gifts. We do things together (painting, shopping, cooking, cleaning, studying) and reveal a bit of ourselves to the other. Just as a picture is worth a thousand words, so too is a touch. For instance, a hug can say: I love you; I accept you for who you are, including all your faults; I encourage you to keep on growing; I like to be around you; you are good for me; thanks for being you, etc. The more intimate touches will communicate a more personal union where words are so inadequate. Sexual intercourse is both a deep sharing of two total persons (not merely bodies) and a complete revelation of self to self. Only married couples can truly express what this total, exclusive and permanent giving and receiving is all about.

The question returns: Is this sexual act truly an expression of the love we have for each other? Let us begin our answer with what the Christian understanding of sexuality tells us. Sex involves persons who relate to each other and express this relationship of love by means of their bodies. These persons are children of God and they have stewardship over their bodies and their sexual faculty. This faculty is most sacred, sharing as it does with God in giving life to others. In no way is it to be abused. The relationship between these two persons is not a casual, passing acquaintance. It is a friendship that has developed into a deep personal union and a commitment to each other which we call love—not puppy love, not a selfish search for gratification. The two persons express to each other in various ways the love they have for one another. They use gifts; they use words; they use their bodies.

Physical sex, therefore, is the language or expression of love. When discussing this concept with students, I frequently ask the question: "Marilee, what would you do if I kissed you the way your fiancé does?" The answer I usually got was along the lines of shock, surprise, "dirty old man." Her answer, however, brought down the house: "I don't think you could." I forgot to ask if I could try. Seriously, though, whatever answer I got always reflected the fact that there are kisses and there are *kisses*. A father does not kiss his daughter in the same way her fiancé does. The one kiss means fatherly love; the other expresses "on the road to marriage" love.

It is true that we can put into any bodily expression—a word, a look, a kiss, a hug, intercourse—whatever we want. We cannot destroy the fact, though, that these different bodily expressions have meanings all their own. We can express a very deep and total love with a very simple kiss. However, it is hard to imagine how intercourse can be a correct expression of "how are you today?" Our expressions therefore can vary from true love to exploitation of the other for my own self-gratification.

What about self-gratification? Is it all wrong? By no means. In fact, there is gratification in all we do. We all feel proud after a job well done. On the other hand, we are self-seekers and at times pursue things for the wrong reasons. Am I seeking self-gratification or is it truly the result of a job well done? Why am I touching this person (kissing, embracing, etc.)? Look at a mother holding her baby. Is it selfishness or is it to show love, comfort, thanksgiving, appreciation for one of God's greatest wonders, etc.? If my touch were not possible, if I were refused, how would I respond? Or would I react? Would I understand, accept, be thankful for, respect the person? This would be a good response. Or would I pout, feel rejected, "you don't love me," "you would if you loved me," etc.? This would be a selfish reaction. A former student of mine wrote a little booklet entitled *Saying No: The Way To Grow*. In it she relates an episode of her courting days when she and her future husband got very involved physically and then he stopped. "I love you too much; I could not do that to you."

What kind of love do we truly have for one another? Since love and its expressions are fundamentally related, love has to exist in us before it is expressed in our actions, otherwise the latter may be nothing more than prostitution, crutches, counterfeit love, self-gratification, lies, etc. The language we use should mirror properly the love we actually have.

Our basic attitudes are very important. How do we look upon each other? What respect do we have for each other and the sacredness of our sexual faculty? Perhaps a comparison with good driving will help. What kind of drivers are we? We can be good drivers and still at times experience such things as crossing the yellow line, stopping in a cross-walk area, or even skidding on the ice. We can likewise drive carelessly and endanger the lives of others every time we are on the road. Our regular expressions of love tell us a lot about who we are, who we think we are, and how we reverence our partner.

There are no set answers to all the questions that come up in regard to sexual behavior. Personal guidance and individual prescriptions are needed. We are not always unbiased judges in our own situations and often need to be protected against ourselves and our strong physical desires. Prayerful reflection is also helpful: What would the Lord have to say about this? All the great people in the Christian tradition had a tremendous personal relationship with God. For them prayer was a sharing of their all with God. They talked with their Lord about everything; they consulted the Lord before they did anything. No wonder they were great. We find that the same is true in our own lives. I can remember an episode in my life as a young priest. I had been working hard to help this young person change his ways. I was in chapel talking it over with our Blessed Mother. "Mom, I've tried everything I can think of and nothing is working. Surely it is the will of God that this kid see the evil of his ways, convert and live a Christian life." I ran out of breath, or of things to say, and paused. I can still hear her words, "Are you upset because the will of God is not being done, or because the will of God according to Father Kohmescher is not being done?" When we pray, as long as we are sincere, we are led to see the whole picture. We cannot lie to God. Any self-seeking is most likely to show itself.

The above can apply to all areas of sexuality—masturbation, premarital intercourse, homosexuality, birth control, etc. In each case we need to have a clear grasp of who we are, our level of maturation, the various values involved and the challenges Christ may be giving us.

### Points for Discussion and Reflection

1. When is a Christian truly sexually mature?
2. Discuss: I can use only the language of love that demonstrates the kind of love that I am now capable of giving.
3. Is it correct to say (as O'Neil and Donovan do in *Sexuality and Moral Responsibility*) that the only answer to premarital sex that we can be sure comes from love is "no"?
4. Should only the virtuous person make the decision?
5. Select concrete sexual problems and/or challenges existing in your own community and propose a Christian evaluation of the situation, e.g., pornography, premarital sexuality, teenage prostitution, etc.
6. "Lord, is it O.K. if Pat and I have intercourse?"

# Illustration Three:
# Peace and Justice

Peace and justice issues are among the most complicated that exist. So many factors may be involved that we do not see the problem very clearly, and solutions are anything but simple. Because the picture is rarely a clean, crisp one, we have tended to ignore the situation and do not see the moral implications of many accepted practices around us. In this presentation we shall just scratch the surface so to speak in saying a few words about peace and justice in general and then by giving a very sketchy presentation of a few issues with the hope that this will stimulate further thought and discussion.

For many people, peace means not being at war. It is much more than that. If true peace existed, the conditions that could lead to war would not be present. Hence, no war. Peace is the proper ordering of things. Everything is in its proper place and everyone has been given his or her proper due. Notice how justice (giving each one his or her proper due) goes hand in hand with peace. Peace is a very positive virtue and is the foundation for all good human living. It is basic to our nature to live with others, to work with them, to get along with them in peace and harmony. It is only when things are not in their proper place, or when people are deprived of their basic rights, that they get upset and fights may possibly start.

For peace to exist, the rights of all have to be respected. We all have dignity and we all are due respect. We all have rights to life, liberty and the pursuit of happiness. We all have rights to work and to receive proper wages (living family wage, equal pay for equal work). Our property should be respected by all. We all have a right to a decent return on our investments. At the same time, our rights are not unlimited. We are stewards of all we have, but we do not have absolute ownership. We are social beings. Our rights are tempered by our responsibility to respect the rights and need of others. Just how far does this responsibility go? What are the rights and responsibilities of groups of people, of corporations, of nations? Should wealth, property, goods be distributed equally? What does it mean to treat people equally? Equitably? And the questions go on and on!

## Our Daily Lives

It is not too difficult to get very irate over some of the problems that will be treated here, and rightfully so, but why do we pass over the issues in our own daily lives? Remember the parable of the Good Samaritan and all those who passed by the victim, doing nothing? We turn our stereos up as far as they can go and disturb the rights of others who want to study or to sleep. We borrow clothes and return them dirty. We break another's mirror and do not replace it. We pull fire alarms in the dorm at 2 A.M. We party in the neighborhood into the wee hours of the morning, making lots of noise, disturbing the rest of others and cluttering up the lawns with our debris. As students we waste our time and money (or is it our parents' money?) by cutting classes, copying assignments, studying just to get by, watching too many soaps, etc.

We shoplift at the local stores. We change price tags on articles of clothing. We show up late for work and loaf on the job. We think nothing of occult compensation—taking things from work to augment our pay. After all, we deserve it. We make fun of others; we use derogatory names; we play uncalled for jokes on them. We do not consider our neighbor's right to decent language as opposed to vulgarity, obscenity, profanity. We lie; we spread rumors; we do not worry about the reputation of others, including our own school. Is everything in our lives in its proper place? Do we give each person his or her proper due—fellow students, parents, teachers, others?

## Sexism

Have you ever been discriminated against? Do you like to wait in a long line and then, when it is your turn to be waited on, have the clerk or the cashier allow a dozen other people to go ahead of you? How do you react if some of your buddies, with the same qualifications and experience you have, get paid a dollar an hour more than you for the very same work? Do you like people to make in your presence, or certainly loud enough for you to hear, derogatory remarks about your intelligence, capabilities, motivation? If you have experienced such things, you may be able to understand the feelings of many women who have been so victimized by our culture. They have been, and are being, discriminated against both in church and in society. They are not always paid equal wages for equal work. Certain doors are kept closed to them without serious reasons. They are made to appear as second-rate citizens, as imperfect human beings, and not as equals under God and under the laws of humankind. Are the principles of peace and justice being properly applied to their situation? All other forms of discrimination based on race, religion, age, etc., fall under the same questioning and challenge.

## My Property

"This is my land. I have paid hard earned money for this and I can do with it whatever I please!" That is a very selfish statement, and we all know it is not absolutely correct. For one, we usually accept the zoning laws of our community, deciding which lands are for residential use, which for business or industrial use. But it is strange that we are blind in so many ways to the social implications of what we do with our land.

I sell my farm to a developer and make a killing on it. After a few such farms are converted into residential or industrial areas, the tax authorities reevaluate the land and raise the taxes on all the property in the area, including the neighboring farms.

Some farmers are then driven into bankruptcy by the exorbitant taxes.

I have several free-flowing springs on my property which form a sizable creek that helps to water quite a few gardens of my neighbors as the creek winds its way down to the river. May I say that the water is mine, dam it up, and use it all for my land, not letting a drop flow onto a neighbor's farm? Minerals (e.g., coal, oil) have been discovered on my property. May I mine these without any consideration of the impact it might have on my neighbors? May I turn my small lot in this nice residential neighborhood into a junk yard? Do I have any obligations to see to it that my house and my yard are kept in good condition?

In our use of all our resources—land, water, minerals, etc.—do we need to consider what they will be like fifty years from now? Are we responsible for the conditions that might exist when our grandchildren are alive? Are we permitted to turn our agricultural and forest lands into industrial parks and suburban residences without any thought given to what this does to ecology now and in the years to come?

## Industry

America has long been looked upon as the land of opportunity. Anyone can start off with nothing and end up a rich person. This has been done, but it does not happen to all, and at times it occurs at the expense of others. Let us look at our industries in the 1980's. There is a lot of talk about the impact foreign companies are having upon American industry. These imported products are underselling those that are "made in America." Not only that, but some "made in America" products are of a poorer quality. There are many reasons for this situation, but let us look at one of them that we did have some control over. In almost every industry the forces of capital and labor have teamed up and entered into contracts that were beneficial to both. Management wanted to turn out a good profit for the investors and labor sought the best possible wages for the workers. Both of these were commendable goals, but look at what happened  When capital takes out all the profits it can and labor the highest possible wages, what is left for plant improvement? Little or nothing was poured back into some industries. Plants and equipment were allowed to become antiquated. As a result either inferior products are turned out, or the plant is closed down because it is uneconomical to continue. Decisions made by both capital and labor over the years did not take sufficiently into account the rights of the plant itself to improvement. As a result the company is unable to compete with others and when it closes quite a few people are out looking for another job. Is this the application of peace and justice?

## World Hunger

Each night more people go to bed hungry than go to bed with a good meal under their belts. We have a difficult time grasping this. Many students tend to laugh (at first) when I tell them this: "Over half the people in Latin America will not *once* in their entire life, not at Christmas, nor on a birthday, nor at a wedding, have a meal that is as good as the one you will eat in the cafeteria today." We are spoiled by our high standard of living in this land of opportunity. We have a hard time understanding that there are many people out there, through no fault of their own and usually in spite of all their best efforts, who go to bed hungry day after day after day.

We are slow to react, whether it be to the plight of farmworkers (especially the migrant farmworker) here in the United States, exploited by their employers, or to that of the third world peoples who starve while they are forced to grow food for the United States. Meanwhile American farmers are paid not to grow certain crops or to plow them under and tons of food are stored in warehouses through the country.

The solution is not all that simple. However, it is evident that, when there is food on this side of the street and there are people across the street starving, changes have to be made. These must occur both in business, where large corporations exploit third world peoples and contribute at least indirectly to their starvation, and in politics, where our American foreign policy seems to have forgotten the ideals that motivated the founding of this nation. You will never have peace without justice. When people have little or no security—no food to eat, no land to call their own—they are not at peace. They are restless; they strive after something better. After a while the human volcano can erupt. Social injustices, repeatedly ignored by so-called democratic peoples, can breed an atmosphere in which the individuals are willing to try other than democratic ways in order to attain more personal security for themselves and for their families.

## The Arms Race

Christian peace should be based on Christian justice—justice for individuals and justice for nations, both large and small. Today the arms race seems to say that the only way to achieve peace is to have more guns, more destructive power than the other. Such a race will never end of itself since one of the major powers will always be striving to outdo the other. This will probably not lead to peace and it could lead to war. The more guns you have, the easier it is for an accident to happen.

What is the basic premise of the arms race? That might makes right? That we need to be able to defend ourselves? That only by having an overkill capacity can we protect ourselves? (Currently we have the power to destroy every Russian city not once, but many times over. How often do you have to destroy the same city?) That we get along best with our neighbors when we *develop* attitudes of trust, care, concern and respect for one another?

What sense of values is reflected in this race? Do we truly put our resources where our values are? Why do we spend more money on guns than on the needs of people? I personally often wonder what would happen if the United States, instead of supplying arms to certain Latin American countries, had taken the same amount of money, bought land from the rich landowners and distributed it to the landless. Is such a dream just that—a dream—or would it produce a better chance for peace and justice to flourish?

The arms race is a most serious one and its proper resolution is key to what kind of a future there will be for our children and grandchildren. The answer, we repeat, is not going to be simple, nor easily attained, but something needs to be done. Where do we start?

## What Can I Do?

There are no easy answers to any of the above issues. To be a good Christian today, however, we do need to respond to the challenges these problems present to us. Among other things, our creative responses would include the following:

a. Peace and justice issues are complex. This does not mean to give up. What we must do is grow in our understanding of the problem, its various sides, its challenge, its possible solutions, etc., by study and by dialogue with others. We need to be open to the total picture.

b. You cannot give what you do not have. If Christian solutions are to be arrived at, we ourselves need to develop strong Christian personalities. The teachings of Christ must become a regular part of our daily living.

c. There is a ripple effect in all that we do. If our families and local communities become models of peace and justice, this will have an impact upon others. If I clean up my yard, plant some flowers, paint my house and talk my two neighbors into doing the same, will this cause others to do some thinking about cleaning up the neighborhood?

d. Be positive in all you do. The bumper sticker reads: Hugs not slugs! We get further by doing something positive than just by bitching about what is wrong. See the problem and take positive steps to do something about it yourself or to join with others in some group response.

*Points for Discussion and Reflection*

1 What are my obligations as a stockholder in a corporation that engages in un-Christian business practices?

2. What obligations do peace and justice impose upon us as educated voters?
3. Are Church-related institutions, such as schools and hospitals, obliged to practice social justice?
4. What responsibility do the media have in presenting all sides of social justice issues?
5. Are the high salaries paid to athletes, entertainers, presidents of some businesses, etc., in accord with the principles of peace and justice?
6. Are today's many lawsuits against doctors, businesses, other individuals, etc., all in accord with the demands of justice?
7. Is it correct for politicians to seek favors for their constituencies at the expense of others?
8. Do we as individuals have responsibilities toward a clean environment or is it only that of the large corporations?
9. What practices in your own community appear questionable in the light of the demands of peace and justice?

# Selected Readings

Curran, Charles E. *New Perspectives in Moral Theology.* Fides, 1974.

Daly, Robert J. *Christian Biblical Ethics.* Paulist, 1984.

Egan, John with Paul Colford. *Baptism of Resistance, Blood and Celebration.* Twenty-Third Publications, 1983.

Gaffney, James. *Newness of Life.* Paulist, 1979.

―――. *Sin Reconsidered.* Paulist, 1983.

Gallagher, John. *The Basis for Christian Ethics.* Paulist, 1985.

Hanigan, James. *As I Have Loved You.* Paulist, 1986.

Haring, Bernard. *Free and Faithful in Christ.* Vol. 1, *General Moral Theology.* Seabury, 1978.

Harrington, Jeremy. *Conscience in Today's World.* St. Anthony Messenger, 1970.

Houghton, Rosemary. *On Trying To Be Human.* Templegate, 1972.

―――. *Why Be a Christian?* Paulist, 1968.

Keane, Philip. *Sexual Morality.* Paulist, 1977.

Kennedy, Eugene. *If You Really Knew Me, Would You Still Like Me?* Argus, 1975.

―――. *A Sense of Life, A Sense of Sin.* Doubleday, 1975.

Larsen, Earnest. *Good Old Plastic Jesus.* Liguorian, 1968.

Lohkamp, Nicholas. *The Commandments and the New Morality.* St. Anthony Messenger, 1974.

Maguire, Daniel. *The Moral Choice.* Doubleday, 1978.

McCabe, Herbert. *What Is Ethics All About?* Corpus, 1969.

McDonagh, Edna. *Gift and Call.* Abbey Press, 1975.

McNulty, Frank and Edward Wakin. *Should You Ever Feel Guilty?* Paulist, 1978.

Meehan, Francis X. *A Contemporary Social Spirituality.* Orbis, 1982.

Menninger, Karl. *Whatever Became of Sin?* Hawthorne, 1973.

Monden, Louis. *Sin, Liberty and Law.* Sheed and Ward, 1965.

O'Connell, Timothy. *Principles for a Catholic Morality.* Seabury, 1978.

Padavano, Anthony. *Dawn Without Darkness.* Paulist, 1971.

―――. *Free To Be Faithful.* Paulist, 1972.

Paulus, Trina. *Hope for the Flowers.* Paulist, 1972.

Powell, John. *Why Am I Afraid To Tell You Who I Am?* Argus, 1969.
————. *Why Am I Afraid To Love?* Argus, 1972.
————. *Unconditional Love.* Argus, 1978.
Saint-Exupery, Antoine. *The Little Prince.* 1943.
Schnackenberg, Rudolph. *The Moral Teaching of the New Testament.* Herder and Herder, 1965.
Sloyan, Gerald. *Is Christ the End of the Law?* Westminster, 1978.
Smith, Joanmarie. *Morality Made Simple But Not Easy.* Argus, 1982.
Van der Poel, Cornelius. *Search for Human Values.* Newman, 1971.
Varga, Andrew. *On Being Human.* Paulist, 1978.
Wassmer, Thomas. *Christian Ethics for Today.* Bruce, 1969.
Westley, Dick. *Morality and Its Beyond.* Twenty-Third Publications, 1984.